Say, is this the U.S.A.

Is it?

Much love from
Anne & Rob
Elizabeth & Margaret

Christmas 1984

**A Da Capo Press
Center for Visual Communication Book**

Series Advisor: A.D. Coleman
Series Editor: Tricia Grantz

Other books in this series:

North of the Danube
      by Erskine Caldwell and Margaret Bourke-White

Land of the Free
      by Archibald MacLeish

Say, is this the U.S.A.

ERSKINE CALDWELL AND
MARGARET BOURKE-WHITE

DA CAPO PRESS · NEW YORK · 1977

Library of Congress Cataloging in Publication Data

Caldwell, Erskine, 1903-
   Say, is this the U. S. A.

   "A Da Capo Press/Center for Visual Communication book."
   Reprint of the ed. published by Duell, Sloan, and
Pearce, New York.
   1. United States—Description and travel—1920-1940.
2. Caldwell, Erskine, 1903-   I. Bourke-White,
Margaret, 1906-1971. III. Title.
E169.C17   1977b   917.3'04'91   77-9958
ISBN 0-306-77434-8

This Da Capo Press edition of *Say, is this the U.S.A.* is an
unabridged republication of the first edition published in New York in 1941.
It is reprinted by arrangement with Erskine Caldwell.

Published by Da Capo Press, Inc.
A Subsidiary of Plenum Publishing Corporation
227 West 17th Street
New York, New York 10011

FOR

The Reverend Ira S. Caldwell

Say, is this
the U.S.A.

Say, is this the U.S.A.

AMERICA today is the scene of a mighty drama, the like of which we have never before experienced. There are moments of grieving and tears, and fits of laughter and hilarity. There are hours of monotonous monologues; there are flashes of fanatical madness. But no matter what is taking place, it is like nothing else that has ever taken place before, because there is no audience to express approval or disapproval. Everyone in America today is on stage taking part.

There are times when it seems as if the scenery has become hopelessly tangled, and sometimes it seems as if the speeches have become hopelessly jumbled. But somehow, regardless, the meaning succeeds in making itself known. As the play continues, its purpose increases in clarity and intensity, even though its ultimate climax can only be guessed at.

In the meantime, there is action on top of action, there is action galore.

The theme of this people's theatre is life in America today. The story is a dramatization of the factory-farm cultural regions, beginning in the

Free Soilers' and Homestead territories, and extending in a semi-circular direction until it ends at the Atlantic seaboard.

Some of the people are engaged in rather strange activities. There are grown men making toys, school children making flags, herpetologists mounting sea turtles, secret fraternal societies re-enacting Bible stories, girls' athletic clubs practicing tumbling, and sheriffs locking up peeping-toms.

Most of the people are engaged in performing commonplace duties. They are making bread, repairing automobiles, teaching school, crushing stone, repairing tracks, punching tickets, selling groceries, digging holes, running elevators, pumping gasoline, and balancing ledgers.

But regardless of whether his life is unusual or ordinary, almost every American today realizes that the small world he once lived in has vanished, and that now he has come to grips with a larger world. He is no longer absorbed, as he was in a recent era, in trying to keep up with the Joneses. He has grown away from a craving for two cars in his garage, and is now more concerned about a permanent roof over his head, his children's preparation for life, and the future of America.

[4]

HUTCHINSON, KANSAS. This America is a jungle of men living in the extremes of good and bad, heat and cold, wealth and poverty. You are born here and you die here, and in the intervening years you take out more than you put back.

Anyone who zigzags ten thousand miles through America these days on train, plane, bus, and horse will find new factories springing up overnight like mushrooms. You will find elevators full and overflowing with wheat, and nobody knowing where the new crop can be stored. You will find farmers who are buying more tractors and more cotton land when there is already so much cotton in warehouses that new ones will have to be built before another year's crop can be sold. You will find families sleeping under highway and railway bridges because there is no other place for them to go. You will find lumber rotting in yards because nobody these days has time or inclination to build houses. You will find wealth and poverty, overproduction and starvation. You will find all these things, and more, because this is the drama of America.

There will be people attending patriotic pageants, dialing the radio alternately between swing music and war news, arguing over bills before Congress, and attending to their business of mining, farming, teaching, and storekeeping.

There will be factory workers making down payments on farms so they will have a place to go when the next depression comes. There will be farmers leaving the land and moving to the

WHITEWATER, KANSAS. The guiding star that led our forefathers from the old world westward over water, mountain, and plain hovers above us still, but our eyes look down at only the small ground upon which we stand.

cities in order to find a job that will enable them to support their families. There will be men, women, and children along the roadside who are neither coming nor going, but who are hoping that the Government will see fit to supply them with food, clothing, and shelter.

There will be boom towns and ghost towns, high wages and no wages, and a shifting of population from jobs that have been completed to jobs that are just beginning, and from there to jobs that will never start.

There will be all these things, and more, along the roads of America, because this is the story of America today.

THE FILLING-STATION CIRCUIT

There was a time not so long past when it was the practice of many well-intentioned writers to make periodic tours of the country's gas stations for the purpose of feeling the American pulse. Assuming that it would be unnatural for it to be normal, they tore over mountains and prairies day and night, stopping spasmodically to inquire of filling-station attendants the current state of the nation. The answers they received, which were duly recorded in their notebooks, were to

FRIEND, KANSAS. You killed off the buffalo by the thousands, robbed the Indian of his homestead, and tore up the sod with fanatical madness. And now in some years your wheat turns to dust, and in other years it springs into a lush carpet of burnished grain.

them statistically, sociologically, and esthetically satisfying. In hard times, the country was going to the dogs; in lush times, it was O.K., America!

I know what the answers were, because I have taken a modest number of such junkets. Probably I would have continued touring the filling-station circuit if it had not been for an incident that occurred in Missouri.

We stopped at a filling station and I asked the attendant if he believed that the patriotism, granting its existence, of the American people would arise to the occasion if a foreign aggressor should threaten the peace of the U.S.A. In other words, if an Asiatic or European dictator came over here and attempted to set up another form of government, I asked, would Americans stand up and fight it out, or would they welcome such a change with open arms.

With a business-like gesture the attendant handed me a neatly printed card. It read as follows:

"I am 36 years old. I smoke about a pack of cigarettes a day, sometimes more and sometimes less, but it evens up. I take an occasional drink of beer. I am a Baptist, an Elk, and a Rotarian. I live with my own wife, send my children to school, and visit my in-laws once a year on Christ-

[10]

ANNELLY, KANSAS.   All these people, all this abundance, all these things, is this America we live in; but none of us knows what to do about it. This is us, this is what we have; but nobody knows what to do next.

mas Day. I wear No. 9 1/2 shoes, No. 15 1/2 collar, and No. 7 1/4 hat. I shoot a 12-gauge shotgun and have a 27-inch crotch. I like rice, sweet potatoes, and pork sausage. I vote for F.D.R., pull for Joe Louis, and boo Diz Dean. I wouldn't have anything against Hitler if he stayed in his own backyard. I don't know any Japs, but I've made up my mind to argue with the next one I see about leaving the Chinese alone. I'm in favor of the AAA, the CCC, the IOU, and the USA. If I have left anything out, it's an oversight. My business is selling gasoline and oil. If you want your tank filled, just nod your head. If you don't want anything, please move along and give the next fellow a chance. I thank you. Hurry back."

We were getting ready to leave when the attendant came back to the car and, pushing his head and shoulders through the window, leaned towards us.

"Say," he began, "I hope you folks don't think I was rude just now when I gave you that card. I figured I had to get up something like that to hand out, because I was being Q'd and A'd to death by people stopping and asking all sorts of fool things and not buying gas, either."

We shook our heads sheepishly.

[12]

LADYSMITH, KANSAS.   In the midst of this country of soil and seed and men and machines is Kansas City. In Kansas City a man is arrested on a charge of vagrancy because he begged for something to eat.

"Anyway," he said, "you folks ought to know the answers to all those questions you go around the country asking, especially that one you asked me a while ago, the one about defending the country."

"Why?" we asked.

"Hell!" he said. "This ain't one of those foreign countries! This is America, ain't it?"

IN AND OUT OF CEDAR RAPIDS

I am certain I would raise the roof if a complete stranger called me on the phone and said, "My name is Soandso and I've just arrived in town. I want to know how old you are, where you were born, and the amount of your yearly income." For many years I have been doing just that. I have found that one word invariably leads to another, and eventually the person on the other end of the wire either hangs up and notifies the police, or else he agrees to carry a rolled-up newspaper in his left hand and meet me on a corner in fifteen minutes.

When we arrived in Cedar Rapids, Iowa, I read the telephone book for half an hour and decided to call the number listed under the name of Mr. Clare Marshall. Mr. Marshall's response

McLAINS, KANSAS. There is little the matter with agriculture that horse sense could not cure. Farmers have been sold a flim-flam scheme to raise foxes by feeding the body of a dead fox to a live one, and then hoping to sell its pelt for profit.

was normally cool. He hung up. While sitting in the lobby of the hotel waiting for the police to arrive, I received a call from Mr. Marshall. He said he had checked up on us and had come to the conclusion that the whole thing was not a practical joke, after all. Mr. Marshall, it developed, is the business manager of the *Cedar Rapids Gazette*, of which his brother, Verne, besides being the organizer of the No Foreign War Committee, was at that time editor.

Instead of answering my question concerning his financial condition, Mr. Marshall invited us to come with him to see a lion. The lion, he said, was not just an ordinary, everyday lion in a cage, but a ferocious horsemeat-eating beast that walked around his friend's house without even so much as a leash attached to him. When we arrived at the house, his friend called out of a darkened upstairs window and said the lion had retired for the night and that it would not be a good thing to wake him up on an empty stomach. He said we should come around in the morning after the lion had had his breakfast.

The next morning we returned, but the lion's master had just left for the bank to make a deposit; that afternoon when we went back again, he had just left for the bank to cash a check. At

[16]

MOUND RIDGE, KANSAS. The hardest part of farming is raising $26.75 a month for payment on the automobile, $3 a week on the radio, and $1.20 on Saturdays for the movies.

least, those were the messages Mr. Marshall brought back to us each time.

While waiting in Cedar Rapids the remainder of that day and during most of the next for a chance to see the lion, we called on Carl Van Vechten's nephew. There were many guests present, and I began talking to some of them about Van Vechten. The conversation was suddenly halted by someone who drew me aside and explained in an undertone that he wanted to inform me in a friendly manner about a situation that existed in Cedar Rapids, a situation sometimes not understood by outsiders.

At that point Mr. Marshall took me aside for a moment and said he had just spoken over the phone to his lion-owning friend, and that there was every reason to believe it would be possible for us to see the lion very soon. Mr. Marshall said the prospects were becoming more encouraging all the time. I looked at Mr. Marshall rather sharply, but there was not so much as the faintest suggestion of a smile on his face.

I turned to continue the conversation with the person who wanted to tell me about the situation in Cedar Rapids regarding Carl Van Vechten, when a young lady dashed up. She said, "I feel awfully self-conscious, because I don't know

[18]

DODGE CITY, KANSAS.   In a certain light, America's cheeks look gaunt and the seat of its pants is sometimes threadbare. But the rest of the time it is a healthy, rip-snorting, slam-bang America slinging freight trains across the country a mile a minute.

what you are going to write. Will it be anything at all like *The Tattooed Countess?*" She suddenly developed a spasm of giggles.

Just then Mr. Marshall passed, pausing only long enough to wink briefly and to nod his head knowingly in the direction where the lion was.

I was all for leaving immediately, but I found myself listening to the explanation of why practically every woman in Cedar Rapids allegedly considered herself to be the original of "The Tattooed Countess"; why the husbands of the city wanted to keep discussion of the matter at a minimum; and, consequently, why Van Vechten visited his home town so infrequently.

Much later I was able to go and search for Mr. Marshall. When I found him, he said it would be a good thing to phone once more to make sure his friend would be at home. He talked for some time over the phone, and finally turned to me with a look of genuine sadness in his eyes, "I begged him to let us come right away to see the lion, but he said it was absolutely necessary for him to go to the bank immediately to compute interest." I looked at Mr. Marshall so hard that I was afraid his feelings had been hurt.

That evening a few minutes before the train left, Mr. Marshall called and said rather breath-

DODGE CITY, KANSAS. Skippers, rail benders, rear stacks, hog heads, tallow pots, smoke artists, snakes, bull snakes, goats, pig snouts, and Mae Wests.

lessly that if we would remain one more day he could practically promise to show us his friend's ferocious lion.

We took the train.

FACTORY-FARM

Year in and year out, the Factory-Farm regions of America present the closest approximation to economic perfection we are likely to know. The pity is that there are only two existing regions of major importance, California and Iowa, and that the natural elements that produced them cannot at the present time be duplicated elsewhere artificially. A healthy runner-up for inclusion in this class is Texas, which is demonstrating signs of remarkable vitality and which may after all some day surpass them in both quality and quantity of industrial productivity and agricultural supremacy. The only fault I have to find with the system that produced these above-the-average conditions is that at the bottom of each of the three instances there can be found a stratum of cheap labor, mostly Mexican, Polish, and Czech, that has been subjected to exploitation.

The two principal reasons responsible for the emergence of the Factory-Farm regions to the

SPEARVILLE, KANSAS. Sheep, cows, hardware, baby carriages, refrigerators, mowing machines, coal, wheat, turkeys, corn, gasoline, mattresses, apples, chairs, pencils, chewing gum, tar, combines, harness, overalls, tulip bulbs, circuit breakers.

positions they now hold are rich soil and skilled labor. A good example of one of these regions is to be found in central Iowa, where factories and farms are situated side by side. Elsewhere, particularly in the Homestead and Plantation regions, is found a great desire to combine industry and agriculture, but little of the natural conditions that will make such a union possible. There is no cause now to believe that America will be in the future anything other than a nation of agricultural regions on one hand and industrial regions on the other, with a well-defined area of Factory-Farms lying between them.

THE LEAN YEARS

On the leeward side of the barn on a cold windswept day the farmer was forking wheat-straw to a shivering herd of whitefaces. The cattle nosed into the straw, mooing as they ate. The silo was empty, and there was no forage. The cows chewed listlessly.

We were out on the South Dakota prairie, two hundred miles from anywhere, deep in the dry wheatlands. Last year's crop had been no better than average, and the one before that had been worse.

[24]

OFFERLE, KANSAS.   They ride through the country in cabooses, and come home every third night. They cook and eat and sleep in cabooses, and come home every third night. They put up a white flag by day, hang a red lantern by night, then they turn around and go home.

"Those cows can't live on straw, can they?" I asked the farmer.

He continued forking straw from the cart.

"What would you feed them if you was me?" he asked, heaving a forkful against the side of the barn.

"Didn't you make any forage last year?"

"Too dry," he said. "Too dry for anything. Too dry for wheat, even if it did make the straw."

The cold prairie wind cut to the bone. Even standing on the leeward side of the barn helped little.

"What will you do if this year's crop dries up, too?" I said.

"Same as I've always done," he said, stopping and leaning on the fork handle. "I've done it for thirty years, and I guess I can keep on for a few more."

"You mean you'll keep on trying to raise wheat?"

"That's right."

The red paint was peeling from the barn, and the dwelling house was sagging and dilapidated. The windmill, jutting high into the sky, creaked and swayed over our heads. Its broken rudder looked as if it might fall to the ground any minute. The fences were down on all sides.

[26]

BELLEFONT, KANSAS. You people of the Homestead Region and Free Soilers' Territory, you are the backbone of America. You make our bread and raise our wool. Sometimes we pay you, sometimes we don't.

In the wheat country it was not the dry years that turned the Homestead region into a shambles; it was the wet years that did all the damage. The people thought the fat years had come to stay. They overexpanded in every direction. They bought up more and more land. They opened up range when it should have been left for cattle-grazing. When the dry years returned, the land was overpopulated, overgrazed, and overwhelmed. The people were stunned. Many of them piled their belongings into trucks and went westward. Most of them remained behind. They did not have the money to buy the gasoline that would take them to the moist western slope of the Cascades.

"Suppose this year's crop is worse than last year's," I said. "Suppose it's a lot worse. What will you do then?"

"It couldn't be worse," the farmer said. "Last year my corn didn't mature. It didn't even make fodder. But I'll get by this year if I can make a crop."

"You mean a crop of corn and cane?"

"Wheat!" he shouted. "Wheat!"

"There's more wheat in storage right now than the country can eat. Why don't you forget wheat for a while and raise other crops?"

[28]

KANSAS CITY, MISSOURI. Three-year-old Dominie and Dandy Anxiety XLI, four thousand pounds of food on eight legs, taking first and second prizes at American Royal Livestock Show.

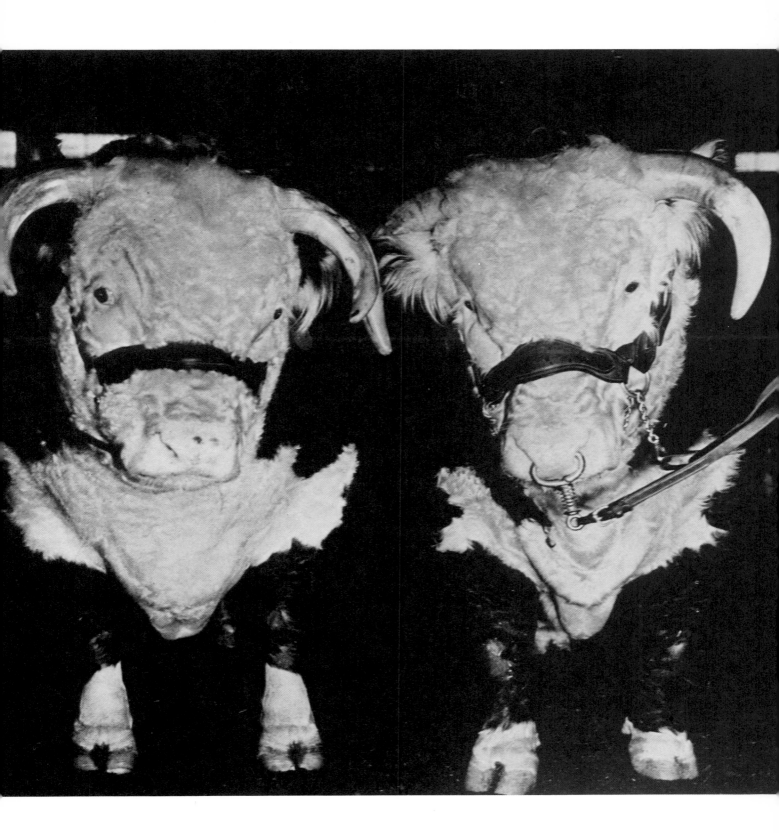

"And have them dry up on me like my corn and cane?" he said, jabbing his fork into the straw. "No, sir! I'm going to raise wheat, or bust!"

THE BOY IN THE BLIZZARD

The train we were traveling on from Omaha to Kansas City was several hours late. An early winter storm was piling up snowdrifts on the tracks, and the engine was at times barely creeping over the iron. It was after midnight when we suddenly stopped. Somebody said we were still at least an hour from Kansas City.

A Negro boy about sixteen years old got on. The train started up after a few minutes, making its way slowly. The boy had wrapped himself in two sweaters, one sweater around his chest, and one around his head. As soon as he settled down in a seat he went to sleep.

The train had gone about ten or fifteen miles when the conductor came through the coach taking up tickets. The boy did not have a ticket, or the money to pay his fare. The conductor without a word pulled the engineer's signal cord. The brakeman pulled on his heavy, gauntleted gloves. The train jerked to a stop. The boy was grabbed

[30]

KANSAS CITY, MISSOURI. Sixteen-year-old Future Homemakers of America, seniors at Smithville High School, taking first and second prizes for canning and milking.

by the collar and hauled protestingly toward the door.

"I'll lend him the fare to Kansas City," somebody told the conductor. "How much is it?"

Several of the other passengers crowded around the conductor. Some of them said it was pretty cold weather to be putting anybody out in, even a Negro. It was close to zero outside, and the fields were drifted deep with snow.

"Putting him off will teach him a lesson," the conductor said. "I don't want his fare."

The brakeman hauled the boy to the door and opened it.

"You'll have to take his fare if he offers it to you," the man said, pushing two one-dollar bills into the boy's hand.

"No, I don't have to take it," the conductor said, shoving the boy through the door and out into the snow. "He's a nigger, ain't he?"

The money fluttered to the floor.

Almost immediately the train jerked into motion, and we began creeping slowly through the frozen night toward Kansas City.

HORSEPLAY

When an American Legion Drum and Bugle Corps takes part in a parade these days, some-

KANSAS CITY, MISSOURI. Fifteen-year-old Future Farmer of America. He knows he must not fall into the errors of the past. He is learning how to diversify his crops, conserve his soil, and improve the breed of his stock.

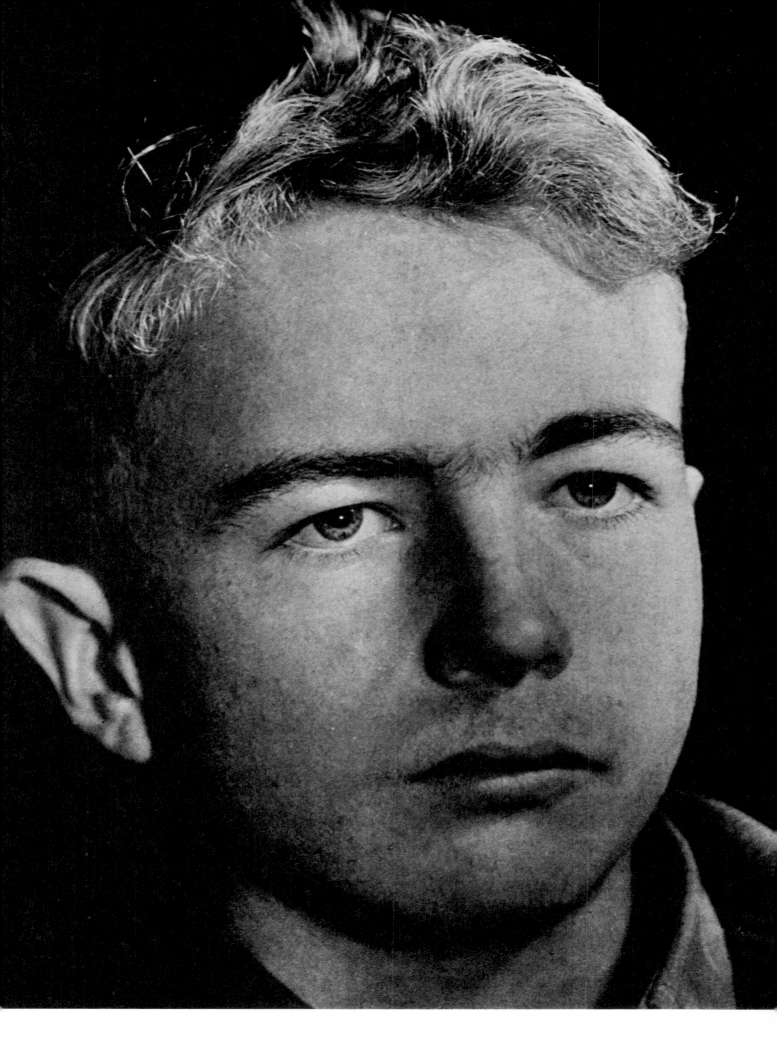

body along the line of march is almost always certain to comment loudly and distinctly in unmistakable terms upon the paunchy appearance of the ex-soldiers. In every instance I have witnessed, the boys have taken the joshing good-naturedly.

I asked a saxophone player in a corps in Kansas City, Missouri, how he felt about going to war again. He said, "I'd fight anybody, anywhere, anytime at the drop of a hat, but I couldn't stoop over far enough to pick the thing up." He had a belly like a barrel.

Two Legionnaires taking part in a celebration in Omaha, Nebraska, were resigned to the fact that any future war America might become involved in would probably have to get along without their active services, but that there were still plenty of ways they could help the country at home in time of need.

But what Legionnaires in any American city lack in physical fitness after all these twenty-odd years of desk-polishing and chair-warming they make up for in horseplay at their Forty-and-Eight gatherings and in horn-tooting at festive events.

I saw a serious-looking business man pour a pitcher of ice water into the coat pocket of a stern-appearing attorney at a Forty-and-Eight meeting;

[34]

BROADLAND, SOUTH DAKOTA. Grasshoppers and foreclosures, bumper crops and tractors, dust storms and droughts, two-dollar wheat and twenty dollar hogs, Russian thistles and politicians.

on another occasion I saw a minister crawl the entire length of a banquet hall on his stomach and give a congressman a magnificent hot-foot; and at still another Forty-and-Eight conclave I observed a dignified-looking mayor gravely sprinkling a generous portion of sneezing powder around the hall.

The Legion's Drum and Bugle Corps, however, can still make the loudest music in America, and they have trained the best-looking majorettes the public is likely to see for a long time.

A BUNDLE FOR BRITAIN

A young woman was sitting in the corner of the hotel lobby knitting a sweater. She had been there for an hour, calmly knitting and paying no attention to the people who passed in front of her. At her feet was a small bag about the size of a portable typewriter case, and from it she unwound the yarn for the sweater. The bag was lettered "A Bundle for Britain."

The lieutenant-colonel, cavalry corps, U. S. Army, crossed the lobby. We shook hands and sat down.

"The Italians don't want to fight," he said quickly. "If they wanted to fight, they would.

[36]

WOLSEY, SOUTH DAKOTA.   Last summer the grasshoppers ate up all your cane and corn, and you hope it gets wetter so they will not work at it so hard this year.

The French wanted to, but their army was shot through with subversive ideas, and the rest was easy. Russia is a giant. Whether Russia wants to fight or whether she does not want to fight, does not really matter. You've seen a strapping big boy walk on a playground and knock the heads of two smaller boys together, haven't you? Well, does it matter in the end what Russia wants or does not want? She can knock heads together."

The colonel turned partly around in his chair and saw the young woman with the bag marked "A Bundle for Britain" for the first time. He stared at her for several moments as though his thoughts had suddenly changed their course.

"Germany has the greatest military machine of this or any other age," he said. "It is the greatest fighting organization in the world. Why argue? It's there, and anybody who looks at it with his eyes open can see it. England is putting up a great fight, to be sure. She may even win this war before we're done with it. But how in the name of common sense can you throw a monkey-wrench into a machine when you can't get close enough to heave it at the thing? There is, so far, no protection on God's earth against night air raids. Slinging monkey-wrenches in the dark at something you can't see is a damned unreward-

[38]

VIRGIL, SOUTH DAKOTA. This is the joy and sorrow of your life. Dry-farming, you live in hope of winter rain and snow, because you know under the blazing sun of summer there is no hope.

ing occupation. But let's get back on the ground. That's where battles are won and lost."

The young woman reached down into the bag and untangled the yarn.

"Before you can make a soldier out of a boy you have got to make him want to be one, and before he can be of any value to an army he has got to have experience. Germany has spent the past twenty years making her youth want to fight, and at the same time teaching them how to do it. The Italians have not had this training. The French had it to a limited extent, the British even less. And Americans, God help us, have not had enough training in the first phase to make the second phase worth mentioning. We still don't have it."

He paused and passed around cigarettes.

"That's why it is now and will continue to be for a long time to come a one-sided contest every time the German Army goes up against a new contender. We can build first-class fighting troops in the United States, and when we are through it will be the best fighting outfit in the world, but we won't have it ready tomorrow. We are just getting around to making our boys want to be soldiers—twenty years behind the world's finest military machine."

[40]

BYRON LAKE, SOUTH DAKOTA. There is a new colonial America; there are colonies within the nation. Hutterians live on collective farms, pass their own community laws, and follow their racial customs.

The colonel stood up, glancing at the young woman in the corner.

"It takes time," he said slowly, "to transform a ball of yarn into a sweater with knitting needles. Wouldn't you think in these days that when an urgent need exists for anything, people would realize that practically everything can be made more quickly and efficiently by machine?"

The young woman glanced up as the colonel departed, her eyes following his erect, muscular figure as he crossed the lobby. After he had gone, she reached down to the bag and lifted it to her lap, placing it in such a position that the wording on it was more clearly visible than before.

STREET-CORNER EVANGELIST

"God damns people who don't stop sinning when they have a chance like this to give it up. Hell-fire and damnation is what He slips them when they walk off and won't listen. He says, 'Hit the road, you bum.' He don't want nothing to do with you wise guys who think you know all the answers. Saving sinners has been His job a long time before you ever was born. You'd better pay some attention if you want to get to heaven. He runs a streamlined train with parlor-

BYRON LAKE, SOUTH DAKOTA. Three girls in a Hutterian colony studying their German lesson. When they have completed their schooling, their governor will arrange with the governor of a neighboring colony for three Hutterian bridegrooms.

car seats up there every day, and you'd better speak up and make a reservation if you want to go. They serve seven-course meals on that train, too. At night they make up a fine berth with plenty of blankets and clean sheets for you, and in the morning the porter comes around and whistles a tune to wake you up and sticks a fifty-cent cigar into your mouth with the compliments of God Himself. Now, ain't that something! I ain't kidding you. Why would I want to kid you? You know it's the truth, just like you know it's the truth about the freight you'll have to hop if you go the other way to hell. Walk on off and put the touch on the town for half a dozen drinks of gin and grab yourself a woman if you want to, but don't think God gives a damn for you if you pass up a chance like this. He ain't got time to waste arguing with you. Take it or leave it, is what He says. I know, because that's what He told me, and I grabbed quick while the offer was out. That's why I'm on my way to heaven with a reserved seat on that streamlined train. I know a good thing when I see it. I ain't like people who ain't got enough sense to dodge the devil when they see him coming a mile off. Go on down the street and put the touch on the town for your gin if you want to, but don't come

[44]

BYRON LAKE, SOUTH DAKOTA. The foreparents of this little Aryan girl had to flee from Austria to Russia two hundred years ago in order to preserve their religious and political freedom.

bellyaching around God in the morning if He tells you all the seats are taken up on that streamlined train to heaven."

SMOKE ARTISTS AND RAILBENDERS

After having used every available means of transportation, I have come to the conclusion that the railway parlor car is an institution created by one of nature's evolutionary processes for the segregation of dull people; and that the freight train was devised for the exclusive use of the liveliest people on earth.

Freight-train riding is a luxury that can be indulged in only by a fortunate few with grit and determination. It is a custom recognized by law west of the Mississippi River, where a man has the right to choose the company he keeps. Freight-train riders will share a boxcar with you without giving you a hard look if your foot accidentally touches a portion of their domain. They will tell you what the weather was like in Galveston without telling you how bad business was. They will tell you how much money they made on a job in Denver without warning you against telling the Internal Revenue Department about it. And if you leave the train before they do, they

[46]

BYRON LAKE, SOUTH DAKOTA. These young Americans, whose Hutterian grandparents left Russia to live in the new world, study English grammar and American history.

will help you roll open the door and give you a hand down without expecting something from you in return.

Smoke artists, skippers, hog heads, bull snakes, and railbenders seem to be far more pleased to have you aboard their ride than parlor-car conductors who invariably suspect you of trying to defraud the company until you prove you have no such motive. The crew's job is to unload a flock of sheep, load a herd of cows, pick up a watering trough, and roll out a baby carriage; but they are never too busy to tell you what time you can expect to reach the next junction.

If you should be asked to ride in a caboose with the skipper, as we were by H. C. Clark of the Santa Fe's Dodge City Division, do not make undue comments about his collection of art poses of the Body Beautiful. He would probably tell you, as he told us, to go hang up your own art poses if you do not like his selection.

CROSSING KANSAS, SUCCESSFULLY

Travelers in all periods of American history have experienced the most extreme difficulty in crossing Kansas. In the earliest times the man who entered the state from Missouri in the east

[48]

PRETTY PRAIRIE, KANSAS. Seedings, births, elevators, wheat, larks, combines, marriages, housewarmings, homecomings, yearlings, burials, tornadoes, tumbleweeds, cottonwoods, jackrabbits.

did so because he wanted to get to Colorado or some place farther west, and not because he had any desire to settle down in Kansas and become a permanent resident. But most men in those days, even the most hearty of them, sooner or later gave up the hope of reaching Colorado after contending mile after mile with Indians, stampeding buffalo herds, and outlaws of the Jesse James school, and became resigned to their fate.

It is only natural that the descendants of these pioneers should harbor resentment against present-day travelers who, with the best of intentions, attempt to make the crossing to Colorado; and, with a certain amount of justice on their side, do everything in their power to keep even those travelers who are on urgent business from reaching La Junta, Pueblo, or Denver.

I have been told that Kansans of the present generation will go to any extreme to prevent the trans-Kansas traveler from making a successful crossing. I am prepared to believe all these tales of fellow-travelers, and yet I prefer, in this particular instance, to confine myself to the facts in the catalogue of our own experiences.

The first morning after our arrival in Kansas we were invited to breakfast by the family that

PRETTY PRAIRIE, KANSAS. Tom Fellowes put a new roof on his home. A. P. Riley has his new house all ready for the plasterers. Ben J. Fuller fell from a ladder Thursday while painting his house.

evidently had been delegated to give us the primary, or wheat-cake, treatment. After eating I don't know how many stacks of cakes, accompanied of course by cane syrup and country sausage, we found that it was impossible for us to get to our feet and leave. We undoubtedly would have eaten in the end just as many stacks of wheat-cakes anyway, but in order to be on the safe side, our hosts had hypnotized us so that we believed, as soon as we finished each successive stack, that we were just getting ready to eat our first one.

During the afternoon a group of poets, writers, musicians, and artists called. We sat far into the evening being lulled into a state of suspended animation by readings of poetry and stories, by recitals of compositions rendered upon string and wind instruments, and by having our portraits and busts done in oil, water color, charcoal, clay, and linoleum.

It was midnight when we finally fell asleep. We were too weary to even dream of getting to Colorado.

Sometime between then and dawn we were called to the telephone by somebody who said he represented a civic organization in a city near-by, the name of which sounded like Darnit. Natu-

PRETTY PRAIRIE, KANSAS.   Elaine Bower was bitten by a spider and has been very ill. The Stitch and Chatter Club entertained their families at a masquerade party Friday evening. Mrs. Lena Phillips has bought a Marimbaphone, and she is learning to play for her own amusement.

rally, we suspected it was all part and parcel of the scheme to prevent us from ever setting foot in Colorado, but our senses were so badly numbed that we were unable to raise a voice in protest. During the remainder of the night we sat at the phone and listened to how many miles of paved streets there were in Emporia, how many gallons of water there were in the Hutchinson reservoir, how many bushels of wheat there were in the Salina elevators, and what was the size shoe worn by the average male, over twenty-one, in Topeka.

By noon the next day we were desperate. And then with what we feared would be the last intelligent use we would have of our wits, we plotted a plan of escape. We walked backwards through the streets to the railroad station, creating in the minds of our captors the illusion of arriving, and there boarded a westbound train.

As far as I know, we were the last travelers to make a successful crossing of Kansas.

THE FIRST WILD WOMAN TO SET FOOT IN
    AMERICAN FORK

We overshot Colorado a good two hundred miles, and found ourselves before dawn one near-zero morning in Utah.

PRETTY PRAIRIE, KANSAS. You yearn for the old days when the people rode you out of town on a rail when they did not like what you wrote in your paper. Even at your age you would rather ride a rail than have to print a retraction for business reasons.

The day before, when we had crossed the Kansas-Colorado border, M.B-W. had asked to see the map. She studied it closely for the next half-hour. Then she laid it aside with a far-away look in her eyes.

"I've found it," she announced mysteriously.

"Found what?"

"The place we are going to next."

"Where would that be?" I asked.

"American Fork, Utah!" she stated.

"Why?"

"The name! A place with a name like that is bound to be interesting. It's the perfect place for us. I'll bet nobody ever thought of going to American Fork!"

"You mean we'll be the first white people to set foot in American Fork?" I asked.

"You just wait and see," she said. "You'll be glad I picked it out when you see it. It's going to be a marvelous place for us."

"Don't you think we ought to think about it a little more before deciding?" I asked. "We set out on this trip to be wild-eyed tourists, and not to do a thesis on the value of place-names in contemporary American civilization."

"Don't you see?" she said. "It's almost like being pioneers and traveling in a covered wagon."

[56]

PRETTY PRAIRIE, KANSAS. After your day's work in garage, field, and store you put on your costumes, administer the devotions, and play poker when the ceremony is over.

The conductor who took up our tickets that evening expressed great interest in the situation. He said he would have to stop the train the next morning and let us get off at American Fork, because the railroad had sold us the tickets, but that if we wished to we could pay him the additional fare and ride to Salt Lake City. M.B-W. firmly declined his offer.

At four o'clock the following morning we were awakened by the Pullman porter who said that we would have to get up if we still intended getting off at American Fork, but that we could go back to sleep if we had changed our minds. M.B-W. told him she had not changed her mind and, furthermore, had no intention of changing it. We got up.

The conductor came into the car after a while and said we were approaching our destination. I glanced out the window. All I could see in the darkness was swirling snow. In a few minutes we stepped out on the hard, ice-crusted ground.

The porters, baggagemen, brakemen, and conductor waved to us as the train disappeared in the darkness. There was nobody in or around the station, and the doors were locked. We thought we heard a cowbell tinkle somewhere in the distance.

[58]

PRETTY PRAIRIE, KANSAS.   Your womenfolk will never understand what it is about your fraternal society that makes going to your lodge hall more interesting than going to church on Sunday.

"This must be American Fork," I said, pacing up and down in the snow and blowing into my hands.

"Shut up!" M.B-W. said grimly.

"I wonder why they named it American Fork," I said. "If they were really going in for indigenous names, why not Siberian Icepick?"

There was no reply, because just then I went into a feet-first glide down the length of the station platform.

After piling our baggage in the doorway of the building, we started out in search of a taxi. There were no lights to be seen anywhere. After going about half a mile we found a street. There were dim outlines of houses on each side, but no hotels or restaurants. We kept on. Dawn began breaking dimly over the towering Wasatch Mountains ahead.

We still could find no lighted dwelling, but we did see smoke coming from a chimney farther down the street. Hoping to find a telephone, we walked cautiously around the house. I climbed up on a box and looked through a window. Pressing my nose against the pane, I found myself staring into a woman's frightened face. I was sure I heard the 'click' of a pistol being cocked. I jumped and ran.

[60]

OMAHA, NEBRASKA. You beat your plowshares into guns, your guns into saxophones, and now you'll have to beat your saxophones back into guns again.

We continued down the street for several blocks and at last saw a light in a house. We went to the back door and asked a man who was carrying wood into the kitchen if we could use his phone to call a taxi. He said he had no telephone, but that the hotel was only four blocks farther down the road. We hurried toward the hotel.

The clerk was asleep. He got up and looked at the clock and said he had no vacant rooms.

"What do you expect us to do, sleep on the street?" M.B-W. asked him.

"Lady," he said, "it's none of my business what you do, but if I was you, I'd see the Government. They might build you a house and furnish it, too, all free. That is if you don't mind waiting an hour or so for them to get it all ready for you."

"We came here to take pictures," she replied, "not to pick a fight."

"I'm sorry, lady," he said, "but you're too late. There was a crew here all last week taking pictures, and everybody in town's already got one."

"That doesn't bother us," she said.

"Have you got the coupons?" the clerk asked.

"Coupons for what?"

"The kind you pass out to people entitling

PROVO, UTAH.   Bicycle tires and sprockets, mortgage loans and discounts, yard goods and notions, building supplies and paint, burial shrouds and caskets, bedroom suites and carpets, patent medicines and sodas, hunting rifles and decoys.

them to have their pictures taken, plus fifty cents, or whatever it is you charge."

"We forgot to bring the coupons along," I said. "How about some breakfast?"

He shook his head.

"My wife's still asleep, and I always let her lay in bed till seven o'clock."

It was only five-thirty by the clock on the wall.

"That's all right," I said. "We'll go to a restaurant."

"There ain't none. This is the only eating place in town."

M.B-W. came forward and laid some of her things heavily upon the desk.

"Please call us a taxi," she said to the clerk.

He shook his head slowly.

"There ain't none, lady," he said, smiling.

"You don't have to laugh about it!" she said.

"Lady," the clerk said, "it still ain't none of my business, but if it was, I'd say something's made you as mad as a wet hen. Why did you come to American Fork at all if it was going to make you so upset to be here?"

"But the name is wonderful," she said, glancing at me from the corners of her eyes. "I thought ——"

I nodded sympathetically.

[64]

PROVO, UTAH. Your city is the finest spot on earth, you would not live anywhere else in the world, and you cannot understand why everybody else does not want to come here to live.

"Sure, lady, I know," the clerk said, "but some day you'll find out that names don't mean a God damn thing in this country. That's the very same reason why I came here myself eleven years ago from Montana. And now just look at the fix I'm in!"

M.B-W. snatched up her things from the desk and walked quickly to the street, slamming the door behind her. I followed at a distance.

THURSDAY LUNCH

At noon every Thursday in the year hundreds of thousands of Americans drop whatever they happen to be doing at the time and hurry to the weekly luncheon of their service clubs. They pile into hotels, restaurants, and tea rooms from Seattle to Miami, slap one another on the back, pin on jumbo name-plates, call each other by their first names, and sit down to eat meals that have done more to safeguard the institution of marriage and the art of homecooking than anything else in the world's history.

I have attended hundreds of Rotary, Kiwanis, Lions, and Exchange luncheons in the line of duty, and I have found that the typical meal, whether in Augusta, Maine, or in Calexico, Cali-

[66]

PROVO, UTAH. You came out in covered wagons, you watered the land; you laid street car tracks, you established the law. Now you pay taxes and conduct business as usual.

fornia, consists of tinny-tasting tomato juice;
wilted lettuce with a dab of slightly rancid cot-
tage cheese; breaded veal cutlet, which if stitched
to two or three dozen other cutlets would make
excellent saddle leather; waterlogged custard pud-
ding; and a dark brown, lukewarm liquid that
tastes as if it were an extract of moulded oak
leaves.

Fortunately, many service clubs provide song
books and a piano for the members who cannot
stomach the victuals, and choral singing helps
pass away the time. In Provo, Utah, after a Rotary
luncheon, Clayton Jenkins took us out to a fine
turkey dinner. Mr. Jenkins, a Latter Day Saint, is
secretary of the Provo Chamber of Commerce,
and it is his job to supervise the repainting of
posters advertising the cultural and business ad-
vantages of his city; to visit members of the
Chamber at their stores and offices; and to sell
canny home-office executives the money-making
possibilities of the Provo trade area. But after
hours, Jenkins is an authority on the American
short story. When he buttonholes you, he will
give you a thorough analysis of the editorial
acumen of Whit Burnett and the editor of *The
O. Henry Memorial Prize Stories*. He is immune
to the fever of collecting first editions and auto-

[68]

PROVO, UTAH. The campus of Brigham Young University where the
sons and daughters of Latter Day Saints dance and ski, and study classical
literature and the books of Mormon faith.

graphed copies; he is enraptured with the fiction form for its own sake; and his library contains twenty thousand short stories.

SON

An elderly man and his son stood at the desk in the telegraph office. The boy, in his early twenties, was writing a message to send his mother back home in Wyoming.

"Tell her everything's going fine," the father said. "She'll be pleased to hear that."

Several other persons came up to the desk.

"He's going to make a fine soldier," the boy's father said proudly. "He's enlisted in the air corps to be a fighter. He's already passed his first tests, and now he's on his way to California to take the final one."

"You mean he's joined up with the air corps?" one of the men asked. "To be a pilot?"

"We think he'll pass all the tests," his father said. "We hope so, don't we, son?"

"You bet!" the boy said excitedly.

"He wasn't drafted?" the other man asked. "He volunteered?"

"That's right," the father answered. "We didn't want him to wait until they called him.

[70]

ELKO, NEVADA. In the West between sunrise and sunset you make fortunes and lose fortunes with cattle ranches, copper mines, and stacks of silver dollars.

He wants to get into training right away, the sooner the better."

"How did his mother take it?"

"His mother was right with us from the start. She's as proud of him as she can be. That's why we're sending her this telegram, so she'll know we're this much closer to the place where they give the final test."

"What do you think about it?" one of the other men asked the boy. "Want to fight?"

"I'll say!"

"Why?" the man asked.

"I've never thought much about the reason," the boy said, smiling shyly. "I guess it's just because I want to see to it that my parents are taken care of. There wouldn't be much use in trying to make a lot of money for them while there was danger of something happening to the country. I guess I believed I could do more in the air corps than I could any other way. Anyway, that's how I feel about it."

The father put his hand on his son's shoulder, gripping him tightly. There were tears in the older man's eyes. Neither father nor son said anything more.

[72]

ELKO, NEVADA.   The richest men in town are those who have just bought a herd of white-faces, or who have just sold a mining claim, or those who have kept their gambling houses open for fifty years or more without locking the doors.

THE MAN WHO SAID WE CAN'T AFFORD TO
HAVE PEACE NOW

He had just returned from a ninety-mile automobile trip in the northern part of the state, in Nevada, where he had inspected a copper mine. He stood over the radiator, getting the chill out of his body. There was snow on the ground outside, and rutted ice in the streets.

"You hear them everywhere," he said, "the pros and the antis, all saying get into the war or get out of the war. It looks like everybody in America has lined up on one side or the other, with every one of them willing to have a civil war right here to fight it out.

"I manufacture electrical equipment, things like generators and cable, and all the little do-dads in between. I've doubled my factory space three times in the past year and a half, and in another month I've got to double it again. All because I've got enough orders on my books, both government and private, to keep my factory running day and night for two years.

"I've got six thousand employees now. It's the first time in twenty-five years that I've had more than a thousand. That's me. That's my little factory back there in Illinois. And if there's one like me, there are thousands. What would happen if peace were declared tomorrow?

[74]

ELKO, NEVADA.   The losers take a chance with the rent money, or shake dimes from the baby's bank; they sell the spare tire, or borrow a dollar from the grocer.

"What would happen would be worse than having every stick of a factory in America burning to the ground. There would be more hungry people walking the streets within three months, the time it would take them to use up their savings, than there are streets to hold them. It would be a lot worse than it ever was anywhere in Europe after the last war, or even than it may be right now over there for all anybody knows.

"What I mean is peace between Germany and England. That's what we can't afford. We've got to keep them at war so we can work at building our defenses. It's like a ball rolling down a hill. We can't stop now. The whole country would blow higher than a ton of dynamite if we tried to stop it.

"I'll bet my last quarter that if either Germany or England tried to stop the war and make peace tomorrow, this country wouldn't stand for it. We would tell them to keep on fighting because it was their duty in order to insure a better peace, or some such thing. We would tell them to keep it up for at least two years more, because that's about the length of time it will take us to use up the money that's being invested in our war machine.

"We can't afford to have all that wealth and

[76]

ELKO, NEVADA. On Saturday night it matters very little to you whether you win or lose at roulette or panguingui, because after sheep-herding on the range for a week, or prospecting in the hills for a month, you are going to mix with the crowd and have a good time.

potential profit thrown out the window. Two years from now we might listen to reason about ending the fighting in Europe. But not now. Germany and England have got to keep knocking away at each other, because we can't afford to let them stop and make peace now."

CRAPSHOOTERS PARADISE

The busiest, noisiest, most slambang place on the face of the earth is the bar and casino of the Commercial Hotel, Elko, Nevada.

You could put together the six o'clock Times Square subway rush, a twenty-million-share-day at the Stock Exchange, and bombing practice at Muroc Dry Lake, and you still would not have anything that approaches the bedlam of Elko.

We walked into the casino and leaned against the bar. But even walking into the place was not uneventful: we had to shove, push, and shoulder our way through a mob of people that was satisfied with things as they were.

A battery of thirty-five or forty slot machines *carang-banged* all around us. Pushing expertly through swinging doors that had not been locked, day or night, for sixty years, a man came in from San Francisco, elbowed his way to the bar, peeled

ELKO, NEVADA.   They tell you the way to win is to bet two dollars if you lose one, bet twenty if you lose ten, but they do not tell you where to get the money.

twenty one-thousand-dollar bills from a roll, and handed it to a prospector on the other side of us.

Down at the other end of the casino shrill-voiced women were screaming around a birdcage where fifty-cent bets were taken. Three six-footers from Denver upped their last drinks before starting out on a hundred-mile drive to inspect a mine.

Crapshooters shouted out their lungs for two-bits, four-bits, and stacks of silver dollars. Edward J. Flynn's ranch partner leaned on the bar speaking casually of drives of cattle in thousand-head herds. We stood there feeling that if we waited there long enough everybody in the world would pass by. A shabby-looking miner came in and sold a claim for a hundred thousand, cash on the line.

The quietest games in the whole place were roulette and panguingui, where gamblers merely lost fifty, or won fifty, at the click of a ball or the turn of a card.

I walked over the pangingue dealer and asked him if he ever played the game on his own time and with his own money.

"Sure," he said, "we all do. It gets into your blood. But you can't win. The house is always the winner."

[80]

ELKO, NEVADA.   Dashboard fronts and boot hills, pay streaks and ghost towns, floaters and fancy women, bindlestiffs and divorcees, sagebrush and salt flats, range horses and pipestones.

PROSPECTING

"There's still plenty of gold and silver in these Nevada ranges, and there's hundreds of prospectors out there digging, but you could travel a lifetime in this big country without ever running into one. In the old days when the Comstock was booming they used to come up here in these hills and stake out their claims and go out with all the metal they could carry. It's hard to figure out what they lived on, because there's nothing to eat in this country and water is harder to find than gold. But every time a strike was made anywhere in these ranges, there was a big rush and to hell with water. There's still a lot of strikes made in this country, but nobody pays much attention to them any more. Two years ago a grocery-store fellow made a strike up here and sold his claim to a big mining company for ten million dollars. In the old days when there was a strike like that, the country would boom for miles around. Nowadays it's all big capital and big corporations, and you can't hardly tell the difference."

THE CHINESE ACT

The man we were looking for in San Diego, California, was Dmitri Senoff, a night-club book-

[82]

ELKO, NEVADA. Phoebe Titus, Lady Catherine, Mu Lin, Minnehaha, Little Red Riding Hood, Lady Macbeth, Madame de Farge, Mrs. Wiggs of the Cabbage Patch, The Angel of the Darker Drink, and Charley's Aunt at the Ladies Literary Club.

ing agent. When we called at his office, he was out, and it was his secretary's day off.

However, there were two girls in his office who offered to help us locate Mr. Senoff. The dark-haired girl, a dance instructor, said it was possible that Mr. Senoff had gone to a hospital to visit a boy in a Chinese tumbling act who had been injured in an accident the night before.

Just as she was getting ready to phone, the blonde girl came to the reception-room door.

"Try the Murphy Hospital," she suggested, going back into her own office.

The dance instructor could not find Murphy Hospital listed in the telephone book. She called Information, but she was told there was no such hospital.

The blonde girl came back.

"I know there's a Murphy Hospital," she said emphatically, "because I was flat on my back there once for five weeks. I'll never forget it as long as I live."

"Why not try Mercy Hospital?" we suggested. "That may be the one."

"That's what I've been trying to tell you," the blonde girl said. "I told you to call the Murphy Hospital!"

She left the room, slamming the door.

[84]

SAN DIEGO, CALIFORNIA. You have to spend most of your time practicing old routines and learning new ones, because if you don't another entertainer will come along and get all your bookings.

"I'll call it, anyway," the other girl said. "I mean Mercy Hospital."

She dialed the number.

"Hello, Mercy Hospital," she said into the phone. "Could you put me in touch with a booking agent who came to see the Chinese act that was sent to the hospital?"

The dance instructor turned, looking at us helplessly.

"They don't seem to know what I'm talking about. They said they didn't know what a booking agent is."

"Ask them if Mr. Dmitri Senoff is visiting a patient in the hospital," we suggested.

She laughed.

"They wouldn't know what his name is. He only went to pay a visit to the Chinese act."

The girl from the next room opened the door and came in. She stopped in the doorway and listened to what was being said over the phone.

"Hello," the dance instructor asked quickly, "can you help me find a Chinese act that was sent to the hospital?"

"How about telling them what the booking agent's name is?" we spoke up.

The girl in the doorway turned quickly.

"How would they know him by his name?

[86]

SAN DIEGO, CALIFORNIA. If you get a week's job in a night club near a naval base, you know you have got to be good, or you will be boo'd out of town at the end of your first performance.

This is the first time he's ever been inside the Murphy Hospital."

"Hello, hello!" the other girl said breathlessly into the phone. "Can't you locate a booking agent who came there to see the Chinese act? Yes, the Chinese act! That's what I said. To see the Chinese act!"

There was a moment's pause.

"What!" she suddenly shouted into the receiver.

The blonde girl took a step forward.

"My God!" the dance instructor exclaimed, slamming down the phone. "That was the payoff!"

"What was?" the other girl asked. "What happened?"

"Do you know what those people at the hospital did?" she said. "They connected me with the laundry in the basement!"

NAVY WIVES

The girls who follow the fleet have a difficult time keeping up with it these days. Wife or sweetheart, a girl often has to make her way across some three thousand miles of the U.S.A. the best and quickest way she can. Some who shuttle

SAN DIEGO, CALIFORNIA. If your local booking agent likes your dancing, he will pass the word along and you will get engagements all the way to Denver and back. If he does not like it, you will probably be out of a job for the next three months.

back and forth between the East Coast and the West Coast have train or bus fare; most of them do not.

During the past twenty years, the life of a married sailor in the U. S. Navy was a relatively routine existence. He was based at one of the navy yards, he rented a house or apartment outside, and he could generally be counted on to come home at reasonable times. But not any longer. He may be stationed at Brooklyn Navy Yard today, and tomorrow sailing out of New York Harbor under sealed orders. His wife may not hear from him for several weeks, but she has to remain close at home to receive his message when it does come. A few weeks later he may be heard from in San Diego in a telegram which merely says, "Hurry out here, Tootsie." She has to hurry if she expects to see him before he sails to Honolulu or the Philippines. He may be stationed out there for a year or two.

We saw several navy wives hurrying to the West Coast the best they could. Several were on busses, but most of them were hitch-hiking. Truck-drivers were the most sympathetic and understanding; the larger and more costly the automobile, the more trouble the girls had. They all tried to hitch-hike trucks first, and automobiles

[90]

SAN DIEGO, CALIFORNIA. Four shows a night, seven nights a week; thirty dollars salary, plus five dollars for your transportation. Back in Kansas where you came from that is still a lot of money.

as the last resort. Most of them reach San Diego or Los Angeles or San Francisco in time to see their husbands before they leave again.

They can be found in gas-station washrooms near navy bases, making quick changes out of travel-soiled clothes to fresh ones, before they go into the city to hunt their men. But every so often, a girl will reach the West Coast only to find that "the" ship has sailed, sometimes only the night before. They cannot do anything about it, and they sit down and wait for word. If luck is good, they will start on the long trip back to the East Coast or to the Gulf Coast. If luck is bad, they try to find a job of sorts that will support them while they wait for the fleet to come back to the mainland. We saw many of them on the West Coast looking for jobs of any kind. If they can pass the city health examinations, and can find a waitress' job, they have nothing to worry about. Those who look for work in night clubs as entertainers are usually disappointed, because that field is filled to overflowing these days.

WEST OF THE HUDSON

When I saw him for the first time, he was walking up and down in the aisle of the train and

[92]

SAN DIEGO, CALIFORNIA. You have nightmares sometimes when you dream you are dancing for the shore patrol and not a single one of them smiled or applauded.

peering hopefully into faces of passengers as though he expected to find somebody he knew. Finally, he stopped at my seat.

"I beg your pardon," he said quickly, looking at me intently, "but you don't live out here, do you?"

"Where?" I asked, jerking my thumb towards the Arizona landscape. "Here?"

He nodded anxiously.

"Not as a rule," I said.

He dropped down into the seat beside me.

"Do you happen to be from New York, by any chance?"

"Partly," I answered. "I live there some of the time."

He put both hands over his face and rubbed his skin harshly, much in the manner of a man relieving the fatigue of his body after many hours of hard labor. When he raised his head from his hands, he looked like an entirely different person.

"Why did you ask if I lived in Arizona?" I said.

"I can't stand it out here," he answered quickly. "It's not just this state, it's all of them. They sent me out here on this trip, and it's killing me."

"What's the matter?"

[94]

San Diego, California.   There are a lot of times when you wish you would meet somebody who cared enough to want to marry you, but it seems as if every sailor you meet has a girl back home in Hiwassee Gap, Tenn.

He turned and looked at me queerly for a moment.

"Maybe you've gotten hardened to it," he said, "but it's my first trip away from New York, and I can't stand it. I just had to talk to somebody from back home, because I knew you'd understand." He leaned closer, slowly shaking his head from side to side. "You don't like to be out here away from New York, either, do you?"

I did not say anything just then.

"I didn't think you did," he said quickly. He took a hurried look at the Arizona mountains. "There's nothing but space out here. There's no place to live!"

"Maybe it's merely a matter of being accustomed to living in a particular place," I said. "There are probably a lot of people out here who wouldn't want to live anywhere else."

He laughed.

"Don't you believe it!" he said.

I laughed a little, too.

"After all," I said, "homesickness is something that happens to all of us at one time or another."

"Homesickness!" he said. "Who said anything about homesickness? I was talking about the big expense my company had to go to when they

[96]

SAN DIEGO, CALIFORNIA. San Pedro, San Diego, Phoenix, Tucson, El Paso, Albuquerque, Santa Fe, Denver, Salt Lake City, Spokane, Seattle, Tacoma, Portland, Oakland, San Jose, San Francisco, San Pedro.

sent me out here on this trip. They would have saved hundreds of dollars if all these people out here moved to New York, because then we'd have our market right in our doorway. Where'd you get this stuff about homesickness, anyway?"

"I guess I misunderstood you," I said.

"You don't fool me," he said, winking broadly. "I know what the trouble is. You're the one who's homesick."

He got up and stood in the aisle.

"Cheer up, pal," he said, patting me on the shoulder. "It won't last for ever. You'll feel like a million dollars again as soon as you cross the Hudson River."

SCHOOLTEACHER

Our search for a schoolteacher who was glamorous, good-looking, and unmarried was the cause of considerable trouble for a time in Tucson, Arizona.

We talked a friend of ours into helping us find out who this young lady might be. Each time he phoned, he turned to us with an increasingly upset mind. The people he inquired of demanded to know why he wanted the name and phone number of the best-looking unmarried

TUCSON, ARIZONA. Their fingers are busy throughout one whole year of Girl Scout meetings, sewing the largest flag in town for the Fourth of July parade.

teacher in town; and, furthermore, why he did not stop trying to make dates with girls he was not acquainted with.

After considerable explanation, we were given the name of Marie Richey, a teacher of music, art, penmanship, and Americanization at Drachman Elementary School.

Our friend, for some reason best known to himself, went unannounced into the girls' locker room at the University of Arizona in search of Miss Richey. He came out hurriedly when he found himself in the midst of a dozen or so breathtaken girls under showers after hockey practice.

Finally, however, we found Miss Richey at her school teaching one of her Americanization classes. The pupils were Mexican. They were being taught to speak and understand English by singing songs and answering simple questions. The songs they liked best to sing were "Two Little Indians" and "Two Little Rabbits." The older children sang "I Like Most Everyone" and "I Want To Go Home."

We kept the children so long after class, that finally a little Mexican girl came up to us and said, "I like most everyone, but I want to go home."

[100]

TUCSON, ARIZONA.   They teach Indian, Mexican, Chinese, and Spanish children to speak English in Americanization classes by having them count the birds that flew from the willow tree and the rabbits that hopped over the log.

We were on a plane flying eastward over New Mexico. Our section had not been made into a berth, because we were getting off before morning. In the section behind us was a party of three; a Frenchman, an American, and the latter's grown daughter. They were playing bridge. Everyone else on the plane, with the exception of the crew, had retired.

I dropped off to sleep for a while, and when I woke up, the two men were talking in low voices. The girl had fallen to sleep.

"You should use your influence," the Frenchman said. "A man in your position should use all the influence you can command."

"But I don't have much influence," the American said. "My paper has a circulation of only 65,000."

"That does not matter. You can widen the sphere of your influence more than you believe now. It is your duty to your country. You are a patriotic American. You want to do what is best for your country, don't you?"

"Of course, I do," he replied quickly. "But I am not convinced it is the right thing to do."

"I am giving you the benefit of my experience," the Frenchman said. "I am giving you

[102]

TUCSON, ARIZONA. They like to tell their teacher when their fathers have jobs and are working, but they do not like to talk about it when their fathers cannot find any work to do.

more than that. I am giving you the benefit of the experience of my own country. Now, do you still not believe in what I tell you?"

"Why do you have so much interest in America?" the American asked gravely.

"Because all Frenchmen love America, that is why. We do not want America to make the same mistake France made. We listened too much to the English. The English misled us. They were not our friends. But Germany was. Germany did not hate us, they loved us. They tried to tell us, but the English would not let us listen to them. Germany will not harm any country that is friendly to her, but she is strong enough to crush any country that will not listen to her, even America. So, that is why you should use your influence to tell the people of America that Germany wants to be friends, but that if America refuses to be friends, Germany will crush her like the shell of a peanut underfoot."

There was a period of silence between the two men. The only sound to be heard was the drone of the engines.

"All Frenchmen do not believe as you do, do they?" the American asked after a while.

"Unfortunately, no," he said quickly. "Many still listen to the English, but that is because they still have not learned the truth."

[104]

TUCSON, ARIZONA. It is difficult for their parents to believe that their teachers sometimes wear sox instead of stockings and that they often join in the dancing with the children.

"A lot of them still believe strongly in a free France. There is no getting around that. But I don't understand why you claim to have such an interest in the welfare of the United States. How do I know you are not one of Germany's agents?"

"I am a Frenchman. No Frenchman wants to see America suffer the fate of nations that have opposed Germany."

"Well," the American said, "I'm still not convinced America would go down in a war with Germany. We are pretty good fighters, you know, when we set ourselves to it."

The plane was coming down for a landing.

"We will meet tomorrow and talk more," the Frenchman said, smiling. "I have some photographs here that will help make my discussion clear. They are photographs of the German Army and Luftwaffe in action. They will surprise you. Perhaps the photographs will convince you if my words fail."

"Perhaps," the American said, waking his daughter.

THE SHEEP AND THE GOATS

The most difficult task a man can set for himself is to try to convince an American cash-crop

TUCSON, ARIZONA.   They like to go to school and play softball, but when the fruit and vegetables are ready to be gathered, sometimes they have to go away with their parents to places where work can be found.

farmer—cotton, corn or wheat—that it is good sense to raise a few sheep and to grow a vegetable garden.

Most farmers, especially in the South and West, will tell you that gardening is something for the womenfolk to do, and that sheep-raising is not farming. The sheepmen winning prizes for Shropshire ewes do not think raising diversified crops, in addition to gardening, is beneath them. As a matter of fact, they are most successful when they raise forage, corn, oats, wheat, and vegetables, and none of them thinks that a well-rounded farm can be operated on any other basis.

Most of the sheep raised in America are grazed on western ranges, and there is sufficient pasture land on most American farms to support from five to a hundred head of sheep, but the Department of Agriculture, and particularly the Farm Security Administration, feel as if they have been doing nothing more than butting their heads against a stone wall after all these years of attempting to convince the one-crop farmer that a few head of sheep never did anybody any harm.

The renegades among sheep-ranchers are those who sell off their sheep and install goats in their place. They usually go to that extreme in regions where arid conditions, plus overgrazing of sheep,

TUCSON, ARIZONA. You have much to live for, but so little time in which to accomplish all you would like to do. There are children to be educated, there are homes to be built, and there is bread to be earned.

has left little more than cacti on the ground. The Southwest is the guilty region. I saw too many goats for the good of the land east, north, and west of El Paso, Texas. After two hundred head of goats have grazed over that range, even the jackrabbits leave it in disgust.

ONE OF THOSE FOREIGN COUNTRIES

The Belgian family came into the hotel, registered at the desk, and asked to be shown to their rooms as quickly as possible. The man, in his late thirties, looked tired and nervous; his wife, much younger than he, was strikingly beautiful. Their three daughters, all under ten, were much better dressed than any of the other children in the hotel. The Belgian's English was halting and interspersed with French. After they had entered the elevator, the clerk picked up the registration card and studied it thoughtfully.

"This is the first time we ever had a guest register from Belgium," he said. "We've had several Germans, and a great many English, but never any Belgians before. There used to be a lot of Mexicans stopping here, too. There was even a Japanese once. But for the past year we've been getting people from all over Europe, and at

[110]

TUCSON, ARIZONA. The weight of a strange world your parents never knew now rests upon you and you must learn the use of its new tools that have been put into your hands.

this rate we'll soon have registered guests from every one of those little countries. We even had a Swiss stopping here last week. It looks to me like this isn't America any more. I used to think America would always stay the same, but now with all kinds of people coming here it's bound to change. These new ones aren't like the ones who used to come over here to settle down and become Americanized. They never had any money, and they'd get a job and dig in right away and it wasn't long before they were just as American as the rest of us. But with these refugees it's different. Some of them have big rolls of hundred-dollar bills and take a suite of rooms instead of just one, and most of them dress for dinner, and you get the feeling that they're not going to stay here any longer than they have to. You couldn't make Americans out of these rich ones. They don't want to settle down here. They want to keep moving until they can get back home. That's why I don't know if it's a good thing or not. It seems to me that the United States ought to watch its step. It's getting filled up with these rich refugees, and one of these days we're going to wake up and find it to be just exactly like one of those foreign countries. When that happens, we'll start fighting among ourselves as sure as God made little potatoes."

[112]

TUCSON, ARIZONA. You are training yourselves for the defense of a nation that was founded by your forefathers because of their desire to live in freedom and equality.

The Easterner's idea of a good time is being able to spend thirty or forty dollars in a night club. The Westerner goes to horse and livestock auctions, shows, and exhibitions and is content to sit all day on a sharp rail watching and listening. It may not cost him a dime; it may cost him several thousand dollars if he takes a fancy to a blooded white face.

The auctioneer's chant is the music the Westerner likes best. It goes like this:

"Forty now one forty now one anybody want to make it one make it one make it one forty-one now I got one make it five make it five forty-one now make it five make it five I got two I got two make it five I got forty-two make it five make it five."

The Westerner sits on the rail with the rest of the railbirds all day and all night. Some of the auctions, when the bidding is good, last for forty-eight hours at a stretch. There is a collection of people down in the ring never known by any other name than the boosters (they keep the bidding going, boosting the price); the agers (they estimate and call out the approximate ages of the animals up for sale); the ring men (they call out any blemishes they can detect on horse

[114]

TUCSON, ARIZONA. Long ago you began your training to take part in the progress of America, and now you must put it aside temporarily with the hope that you will live to be able to take up again the task of making America the country it should be.

or steer); and the helpers (they whip up the stock on the ring to make them reveal how lively, or decrepit, they are).

Sitting in the gallery, but more usually on the railing around the ring, are the "sweaters." Sweaters are small-bankroll buyers who sit and stew while the cheap prices prevail. They buy the plugs and the culls at bargain prices and sell them to farmers deep in the country who cannot afford to come to the auctions.

We attended shows and auctions all over the West, and I have yet to see a contract signed or money passed between traders. A nod of the head seals the bargain, and no names, bank references, or certified checks enter into the deal. When a buyer is ready to haul away his purchases, he loads his stock, and signs his check for the amount owed.

There is only one nation-wide superstition prevailing among horse-and-cattle men. On their farms, you will generally find a goat. When you ask one of them why he keeps a single goat around his corral or barn, he will either give you an out-and-out truthful answer, or else he will tell you that the goat is his children's pet, or that he is boarding the goat for a friend. The truthful answer is that he keeps the goat with the belief that

TEXARKANA, TEXAS. They come to the auction with a thousand-dollar pair of sugar mules, stand around the ring a day or two, and go off somewhere with a carload of twenty-dollar plugs. A week later they are back again with another fine pair of mules and five hundred in cash.

goats absorb, ward off, and insure against diseases and ailments common to horses and cattle.

I have asked dozens of ranchers why they keep a goat with their stock, and three out of every five say their horses are kept free of distemper and their cattle free of hoof-and-mouth disease by the presence of the goat. Two out of five say it is the children's pet; but when you ask the children who the goat belongs to, almost without exception they reply sadly, "It's Papa's."

B-GIRL

We were sitting in the night club at ten o'clock in the morning watching the cleaning women polish and dust and rearrange tables and chairs. After a while a bartender came in and went to work cleaning the bar. We went over and talked to him for a while, and during the time we were sitting there a girl came in and glanced around the room as though she were looking for somebody.

"Who do you want to see?" the bartender asked.

"I'd like to speak to the boss," she replied.

The bartender shook his head.

TEXARKANA, TEXAS. They bring in anything with four fetlocks and a whinny and somebody will bid it in. A few days later it will be sold to a farmer two hundred miles away for ten dollars down and a mortgage on next year's crop.

"The boss never comes in until around two o'clock in the afternoon," he said.

The girl sat down on one of the stools. She looked tired and worn; she appeared to be about nineteen. Her clothes were neat-looking, but they were cheap and old. The bartender went about his work of washing and polishing glasses.

"Looking for a job?" I asked her after a while.

She turned quickly, nodding her head eagerly.

"The boss doesn't do any hiring, himself," the bartender said, shaking his head. "Everything around here is on concession. That's how it is."

"Cigarette girls, too?" she asked him, leaning anxiously over the bar.

The bartender nodded, looking at her closely.

"You're no cigarette girl," he said finally.

She dropped her head, making no reply.

Nothing was said by anyone for several minutes. The bartender had turned around and was arranging glasses on the shelves of the cabinet against the wall. The girl moved as if to leave.

"Why do you need a job?" I asked her.

She looked at all of us before answering.

"My husband's in the Navy," she said. "I've got to do something." There was a long pause. "I've got to keep busy so I won't miss him so much. And I've got to earn part of my living, too. He can't send me very much money."

[120]

TEXARKANA, TEXAS. When you want to make a horse trader happy, keep the fancy pacers and trotters outside. What he wants is sawdust on the floor, the smell of alfalfa in the air, a good whip in his hand, and plenty of sugar mules and range horses in the ring.

"If you miss him a lot, why don't you live near his base?"

"He's been transferred to Hawaii. They won't let me go out there."

"You could go home and stay with your parents until he was transferred back to the mainland, couldn't you?"

"I don't have a home," she said quietly.

The bartender turned around and doused a handful of glasses into the water. Nobody said anything for a while.

The cleaning women were wiping dust off the tables and chairs, and two men came in and went to work waxing the dance floor.

The girl turned, biting her lips.

"Do you know where I can find a job?" she asked, her eyes wide and searching.

"I'm not in show business," I said. "I don't know a thing about finding a night-club job."

She looked off into space, her fingers twitching nervously.

"I'm really a B-girl," she said almost inaudibly. After she had spoken, she turned around quickly. "All B-girls aren't bad. People have the wrong idea about B-girls just because some of them are bad. But I'm not!"

The bartender nodded.

[122]

TEXARKANA, TEXAS.   A trader with a sick horse on his hands will make his wife get out of bed in the middle of the night, and put his horse into it, if he thinks it will do the animal any good.

"I thought you was a Bar-girl when you came in," he said. "I don't get fooled very often."

He reached for a dry cloth and began polishing a glass.

"I wanted to get out of it," the girl said. "That's why I came in here looking for a cigarette-girl job. B-girling gets me down. Drinking all that champagne gets us all down. Nobody could stand it night after night all night long. I don't blame some of the girls for doing what they do when they can't stand it any longer. If we don't drink champagne with the customers there isn't enough commission in B-girling to make a living. We can't drink soda pop or ginger ale any more. The customers are wise to that. They won't drink with us unless it's got a kick in it. That's why some of the girls go bad and give B-girling a bad name. They do it just so they won't have to drink all that champagne. But all B-girls aren't bad!"

Nobody spoke. After several moments the girl got up.

"If you hear of a job anywhere," she said, "please leave word at the bar for me. I'll come back after I've made the rounds. I'd rather get a cigarette-girl job, even if there's not as much money in it, because then I wouldn't have to

[124]

TEXARKANA, TEXAS. They are up all day and all night keeping a sharp eye on the bidding, leaving only long enough to eat a T-bone steak occasionally, because they are afraid some trader will step in and make better buys.

drink all that champagne." She took several steps toward the door. "But I'll B-girl again if nothing else turns up."

We nodded as she turned and walked toward the street. At the door she hesitated for a moment.

"If they ask about me, please tell them I'm not like some B-girls!"

We watched her walk through the door and out into the dazzling sunshine.

"If there's one, there's a million," the bartender said. "What the hell kind of a country is this, when the girls have to make a living that way?"

CONVERSATION AT REDWATER, TEXAS

"Lend me a dollar, Joe."

"Ain't got it to spare, Jim."

"I've just got to get hold of a dollar somewhere."

"Maybe your wife's got a little put away someplace."

"It's her that's raising so much hell, Joe. I've got to get hold of a dollar and give it to her."

"Ain't you been working lately? I thought I saw you getting paid off last Saturday night."

[126]

TEXARKANA, TEXAS. They bid forty on a sixty-dollar horse and ten more is easy to get but the next ten is five short so he takes that and asks for another but gets three and then he asks for two and gets one so he asks for one again gets a half and one more half makes sixty.

"That's all gone. I took a little trip off aways after I saw you, and it all went."

"What's your wife want a dollar for?"

"She says she ain't been to the pictures since a week ago Friday and she's been after me since early this morning to give her a dollar so she can go and take the kids."

"That's right, but I just ain't got it to spare, Jim."

SIGN ON DOOR OF GENERAL MERCHANDISE STORE, SARATOGA, ARK.

"Notice to the public: We want to please everybody. We keep our store open 6 days every week the year around, without taking any holidays. We close only for funerals or to go to the storm house in times of threatening weather. Hereafter for our customers' convenience, we will open the store at about 8 o'clock every Sunday morning, and when church is over at about 12 o'clock. It is our desire to rest and go to church on Sunday and we ask that our customers get their Sunday needs on Saturday or at times when we are open, above indicated, on Sunday and not ask us to open the store at any other times on Sunday except in times of extreme emergency."

[128]

TEXARKANA, TEXAS. Foals, colts, yearlings, fillies, mares, dams, geldings, stallions, mustangs, pintos, paliminos, bronchos, cayuses, plugs, jackasses.

JASPER COUNTY CROSSROADS, MISS.

"Which one of these roads goes to Stringer?"
"What you want to know that for, son?"
"I want to go to Stringer."
"What makes you want to go away over there?"
"Business."
"I've got a pretty good line of goods right here in my store. You'll save time and everything else buying right here, son."
"I don't want to buy anything. I'm going over there for other reasons."
"Ain't much to see when you get there, son. It wouldn't hardly be worth your while."
"I thought I'd like to go, anyway."
"It's a waste of time to go to Stringer. The men over there ain't got no money to buy anything with, and the girls are as ugly as sin."
"It's not far, anyway, is it?"
"There are places of a heaper distance."
"Which of these roads goes there, the right-hand one, or the left?"
"Looks like you've sort of got your head set on going to Stringer, ain't you, son?"
"I guess I have."
"You're going over there just to look at it?"
"That's what I want to do."
"The devil take it, I've never had my interest

[130]

Soso, Mississippi.   You cleared the forest, your slaves grew your cotton, and you lived in abundance; the earth settled down to giving you all it was able to give, but for some reason it is not sufficient.

rise up so much before in all my life. I've lived
here at the crossroads sixty-one years, and I ain't
never so much as wanted to go to Stringer before.
Wait a minute while I lock up my store, son. I
want to go along with you to find out just what
that devilish place does look like."

SOUTHERN TOWN

In the South, where State pride is something
to be reckoned with, and where I have known
families that refused to accept opportunities for
better living because it meant moving a few miles
over a boundary line, Mississippi is sometimes
referred to by citizens of neighboring States as
a so-so place.

When we reached Mississippi, we went di-
rectly to the town of Soso. The town had been
dis-incorporated by its citizens for the purpose
of making the State of Mississippi pay for the
paving of the highway through its corporate lim-
its. Lacking a charter, it could no longer have
a mayor; but the people said they did not need
one, anyway. There were no laws to be enforced,
no one empowered to keep order; but the people
said they were not worried over that, because
nobody in Soso wanted to disturb the peace.

[132]

Soso, Mississippi.   There is little use for the train to stop at all now, because it does not run as far as a man nowadays wants to go.

The village had been given its name sixty years before when a storekeeper answered all small talk regarding the condition of business and the state of his health by saying, "So-so." Nearby farmers fell into the habit of going to the settlement where everything was always "so-so." And when the post office was established a few years later, the Post Office Department in Washington thought it was a good idea, too. There is a large consolidated school for white children in Soso; a depot of the Illinois Central Railroad where the station agent and his wife live in dignified surroundings; a schoolteacher who writes lyrics for patriotic songs; an oil-well rigging that has drilled to a depth of 6,200 feet without striking anything beyond a seam of coal at the 4,000-foot level; a Negro school built by the Rosenwald Foundation where the teachers receive from the State salaries ranging from $25 to $50 a month; and a type of soil known to agriculturalists as "Orangeburg dirt."

We spent the greater part of our time in Soso trying to find a composer of religious songs. He was said to have written the music for many of the hymns sung in southern churches, he was generally regarded as being Soso's most cele-brated citizen, and on several occasions we were

Soso, Mississippi. Grinding corn meal for people is not as dignified as working in the bank, but when they come in and talk to you about their troubles, you are glad you can afford to listen without having to charge them a fee.

told that his income from music royalties sometimes amounted to almost two hundred dollars a month. He was such a busy man that we were never able to find him.

NEGRO SCHOOL PRINCIPAL

"I hate to start right in talking about our troubles, but I worry so much about it there are lots of nights when I can't go to sleep at all. My people pay taxes just like the whites, according to the value of property owned, but us Negroes don't get anything at all in return for what we pay out like they do. The county pays me a salary of $50 a month, and one of my teachers gets $40. The rest get $25 a month. The principal of the white school with only a handful more pupils gets $200 a month, and not one of his teachers gets less than $100. The white teachers can save up and go to summer school and keep up with their work and improve their teaching methods, but my $25-a-month teachers can't go because there's no way to save anything out of pay that small. We are barely able to get by at all, and if the Negro families nearby didn't help us out with a lot of free board and room, I don't know what we'd do. The Negro people nearby

Soso, Mississippi. If Tom McNair falls out of his barn, or if J. M. Oliver's wife catches a fox in her cold-cellar, or if Judson Hendricks' daughter marries the mail carrier, you will hear about it a lot sooner at the barbershop than you will in the newspaper.

help out the best they can in other ways, too. They take up collections to let us buy books for our library, and for the other things we need to run a school of close to two hundred pupils. I'm not complaining against the white people for what they've got, because I'm in favor of everybody having the best standard of living he can get. But I think Negroes ought to share better in the money spent for education. It would be the fair and square way to treat us if they would divide the education money collected from taxes so that all children, Negro and white, would have the same chance to benefit by it. Every time I talk to the white people about it, some of them always say my people don't need much education to get along, and that if half the Negro children dropped out of school, we would need only half as many teachers, and then the ones that were left could get twice as much salary. The white people talk like they don't care if we get my people educated or not. But they come around and make a big fuss if we don't pay the taxes when they fall due."

CIRCUS

We went to Sarasota, Florida, to see the circus in winter quarters. The best sideshow on the

Soso, Mississippi. You have never made much money, and you have to do without a lot of things other people have, but you would rather live where you are than move to town and work for twelve dollars a week in a shirt factory.

entire grounds was a four-year-old chimpanzee, "Dizzy Dean," and his keeper, Charlie Tanner. Charlie's official title is Keeper of the Great Apes; but, of them all, he prefers the company of Diz.

Diz wanted to have his picture taken, and he expressed himself in no uncertain terms. After the first ten or a dozen shots, he demanded that it be taken over and over again. Each time Charlie told Diz he had had enough, Diz put up such a pathetic squawk that there was nothing to do but continue. Diz insisted on posing in every imaginable position, and in one or two beyond human imagination. He posed side-view, full-face, back-of-the-head, upside down, hind-quarters, and prone on his stomach. When all the plates and flash bulbs had been used up, Diz still had not had enough, and he insisted on having the shutter of the empty camera clicked while he posed some more. Henry "Buddy" North, vice-president of Ringling Brothers and Barnum & Bailey's Combined Shows, finally put his foot down and set Diz packing off to bed.

When we were ready to leave the circus grounds, Buddy brought out an automobile formerly owned by the Czar of Russia. It was a high-wheeled, high-seated machine that whizzed

Soso, Mississippi. They wonder sometimes why the white children ride in big yellow busses to the big brick schools where there are swings and big hot stoves, while they have to trudge along the best way they can.

over the Florida roads at thirty-miles-an-hour. Not present during the ride was John Ringling North, brother of Buddy and president of the shows, who, his friends say, surprises his feminine acquaintances who go in for gardening by making them frequent presents of his favorite plant food, alligator manure.

THE BOX-MAKER

Disregarding the traffic light, and with head bent against the drizzle, the Negro came charging across the street. Before I could get out of the way, he had bumped heavily into me.

"Say, boy," I shouted at him, "you ought to look where you're going on a night like this!"

He backed away, looking up at me with a broad grin on his face.

"Howdy, boss," he said. "I didn't jar you none, did I?"

"A little," I said, "but it won't matter if you'll tell me how to get to the Roosevelt Hotel."

"That's one thing I don't know," he said sadly. "I wish you'd asked me something I knew all about."

"Why don't you know where it is?" I said. "You live in Jacksonville, don't you?"

[142]

Soso, Mississippi. They would like to have a football, a basketball, and a baseball, but their parents have a hard time just getting enough for them to eat and wear.

"I live under the ground, boss. I don't know a thing about what's on top of it. I've been down there near about two years and I wouldn't be up here now if I didn't have to go see the doctor. The doctor he wouldn't come down there, so I had to come on up here to see him."

The Negro was about twenty-five years old and of medium size. He was dressed in patched overalls and an old gray sweater without elbows. His skin was dark, but not black, and his hair was fairly straight. His teeth were even and white.

"What do you do underground all the time?"

"Nail boxes together, boss," he said. "I've been a box-maker all the time down there. I've got me a little place to sleep, and I don't have to come up on top at all. I've got me a steady little business that keeps me on the move all the time."

He started walking away.

"Wait a minute," I called. "What kind of boxes do you make down there?"

"Coffins."

"You mean you're a coffin-maker?"

"That's right, boss."

I walked toward him.

"How'd you ever get started making coffins under the ground?"

[144]

SOSO, MISSISSIPPI. They grow up just like white children, even playing the same games and liking candy and peanuts, but when they get older they have to stop wanting to do the things white people do.

The Negro looked at me soberly for several moments before replying.

"You ain't the law, is you, boss?"

I shook my head convincingly.

"Back up in Georgia they put me on the chain gang for three years because I owed a white man eleven dollars and I made myself a promise I was going to let the daylight burn itself out before I ran myself the risk of getting in another jam like that one. I came down here to Jacksonville and found me a basement deep in the ground where the daylight never struck and started making boxes, big ones and little ones and all sizes to fit the folks who needs them to be buried in. Every once in a while I get to thinking about the daylight up here and I ask some of the folks when they come to buy a box how it looks up on top. Nearly always they say it's sunny and bright up above, and that makes me stop worrying about it, because I know the daylight's going to take a long time to burn itself out at the slow pace it's going. I ain't in no hurry at all. I can wait it out. When I get restless, all I do is think about them three years on the chain gang, and it quiets me down in no time. Besides, I sort of like making the boxes, and I wouldn't want to give that up, no way."

[146]

SARASOTA, FLORIDA. People come to the circus and stare a long time at Dizzy Dean, and go away saying how much Diz looks like Cousin Hathaway.

I was standing on a street corner in front of the State Capitol in Columbia. It was midnight, and the city was quiet. A few automobiles passed, and occasionally a man walked past. A cold icy wind had driven almost everyone off the streets.

After I had been standing there for about half an hour, a boy crossed the street and came towards me. He was about twenty or twenty-two.

There was nothing said for several minutes. He had stopped several feet from where I stood, and I noticed that he glanced in my direction every few moments. I lit a cigarette and tossed the empty match-book into the gutter. The boy moved two or three steps closer.

"Got anything on for tonight?" he asked in a husky whisper.

"What do you mean?" I asked, wondering what he was talking about.

"You don't live in Columbia, do you?" he asked, moving closer.

I shook my head.

"I thought you might be getting ready to go somewhere," he said. "How would you like to have me go along with you? I've got a car and I know this country pretty well."

[148]

SARASOTA, FLORIDA.   If you have ever tried to train a kitten to walk on a leash, you will have some idea of what a task it is to train the big cats to take their cues and leap through hoops.

"What's up?" I asked, lowering my voice. I still did not know what he was talking about.

"Want to stick up a place?" he whispered. "I know a good one where there's plenty of money. It's a filling station about three miles from here on the highway. I've been watching it. They keep open all night. It'll be easy."

I did not say anything for a while. Several cars passed along the street, and a man came out of a restaurant on the opposite corner and got into a taxi.

"How about it?" the boy asked. "We can make a big haul out there at this place I know about. They've got plenty of money in the cash register this time of night."

While he was talking, I looked at him closely. His clothes were expensive and well-kept, and he wore a jeweled fraternity pin on his vest. I had decided that the boy was joking; but, as I shook my head and started across the street, he gripped me desperately by the arm.

"Let's do something!" he pleaded. "I know another place, too!"

We looked each other straight in the eyes until his hand reached for my arm again. I pulled away from him and hurried across the street. When I got to the other side, I stopped and looked

SARASOTA, FLORIDA. Every bull takes a shower bath with a hose, gets a manicure with a rasp, has a shave with a blow torch, and does his daily-four-dozen-setting-up-exercises.

back. The boy had turned and was walking slowly away, glancing back at me over his shoulder.

While I watched him disappear up the street, a taxi-driver who had been sitting in his cab a few feet away got out.

"Did he sell you?" the driver asked.

I shook my head, wondering.

"That boy's been trying to find somebody to help him do something all night," the driver said. "He's already been in half-a-dozen jams this fall, and if his father wasn't one of the richest men in the state, he'd be in the pen right this minute."

"What's the matter with him?" I asked.

"Excitement, or something. I don't know what's got into him. But he's been that way for about a year. You don't see many of these rich men's sons anymore, because most of them have learned their lesson and gone to work. It's a pity a boy like him is left to roam the streets when all of them ought to be drafted into the Army. The poor boys get sent to the CCC, or they get drafted, but the ones that ought to go are ones like him. He busted out of college a year ago, and he gets a hundred dollars a month allowance from his old man. He hangs around now all the time trying to get in some stick-ups for the excite-

[152]

SALUDA, SOUTH CAROLINA. Writ of estoppel, plain drunk, homicide, involuntary manslaughter, committing a nuisance, brandishing a pistol, resisting an officer, number four-oh-nine, breaking and entry, disturbing the peace.

ment. But times are changing fast. They'll get him in the Army one of these days, if he ain't shot in a stick-up first, and everybody will be better off. This draft came along at just the right time, because if it hadn't come along when it did, this country would have been full of boys like him roaming the streets. If the draft doesn't do any other good, it'll make men out of boys like him. It's my guess that the draft is a sign of the times. It's exactly what was needed to keep this country from going to hell."

THE DEPUTY

The deputy sheriff sat in his office, feet on table, and looked out the window at the iron-barred windows of the jail. A man was standing beside him, counting the keys on a ring. He jingled the keys and put them back into his pocket. The deputy looked around.

"I don't mind going out after a nigger in the daytime," the deputy said, "but I don't like to be called at night when I'm in bed."

The other man leaned against the wall.

"It wouldn't have troubled you none, Ed," he said. "This nigger was no more than a mile away. All you'd had to do was come out there and grab

[154]

SALUDA, SOUTH CAROLINA.   There are quite a few peeping-toms at large, and a lot more beer-drinkers driving cars, but it is much more trouble to bring in white boys.

him. He was hiding in the bushes along the road when I phoned you. It wouldn't have been no trouble at all for you."

"Well, it's just like I said a while ago," the deputy said.

"I know that, Ed," the other man said, "but somebody's got to go out once in a while and get these niggers when they act up. This one I'm talking about was poking around my house looking in the windows for about half an hour, my wife said. If I hadn't come home when I did, he might have made a lot of trouble. Looks like you could've come out there and got him when I phoned about it."

"Well, I'll tell you what," the deputy said. "You just act like nothing had happened, and one of these days that nigger will turn up in the daytime. When he does that, I'll grab him for sure. But I can't be getting up out of bed in the middle of the night. I've got to get my rest."

THE LAND-CRUISERS

Just before dark a roomy convertible coupe with polished light-blue paint stopped at the curb in front of the hotel. Two well-dressed girls, each about twenty years old, stepped out and smiled

[156]

SALUDA, SOUTH CAROLINA. You worked harder than any other citizen to get more square yards of paving and more building-brick per capita than any other town in the U.S.A., and you take delight in the telling of it.

at the doorman. They looked like show-girls on a vacation. The doorman lifted out the four pieces of luggage, and tore off a garage check for the car. One of the girls handed him a crisp dollar.

"Seen a good movie lately?" the taller girl asked him, smiling.

Before he could answer, they went into the hotel. A bellboy followed with the luggage.

On the way up to their room in the elevator, one of the girls asked the operator if he had seen a good movie recently. He was handed a dollar before he could say anything.

When they reached the room, the bellboy opened the windows and adjusted the curtains. When he turned to leave, the tall girl was leaning against the closed door.

"How long have you worked in this hotel?" she asked him.

"About a year and a half," he said.

The other girl opened her pocketbook and took out a dollar. She held it a moment before giving it to him.

"Pass the word around, will you, sonny," she said, putting the money into his hand.

The bellboy moved towards the door. The other girl was still leaning against it.

[158]

SALUDA, SOUTH CAROLINA.   The undertaking parlor, the bank, the court-house, the grocery store, the filling station, the pool room, the drug store, the beauty parlor, the liquor store, the post office, the drygoods store, the meat market, the fish house, and the bus station.

"I can't afford to get into any trouble," he said, looking from one girl to the other.

The girl at the door moved away, crossing to the window. She sat down in a deep chair and put her feet on the bed.

"That goes for all of us, sonny," she said, nodding her head slowly. "Don't forget."

The boy paused with his hand on the doorknob.

"When you came in, I thought you were movie actresses, or something like that," he said. "Then when I heard you asking the other boys if they'd seen any good pictures lately, I was almost certain you were." He put the dollar into his pocket. "We don't get many land-cruisers as good-looking as you girls are. Most of them driving back and forth between California and Florida these days are plenty plain. I guess that's why I was fooled for a while when you came in." He opened the door. "Going to stay here several days?"

"That all depends," said the girl in the chair. "Don't forget to be a gentleman, sonny."

The boy backed out of the room, nodding understandingly.

[160]

LOWELL, MASSACHUSETTS. You have to manufacture your products as cheaply as possible these days, because people want a lot of things and they have to make what money they earn go a long way.

CELL-BOY

The Negro boy sat on a bunk in the cellroom and chewed the end of a match. He was about eighteen years old. He was wearing a pair of faded overalls and a torn jumper. Under the jumper was a frayed tan sweater.

"What are you in jail for?" I asked him.

The boy looked up at me and down again at the floor before saying anything. The corners of his mouth twitched several times in quick succession.

"I didn't do nothing much," he said, moving his lips as though they were heavily weighted. "I didn't do nothing at all much."

"They must have locked you up for something," I said.

The boy got up and walked across the cell and back. There was a high window overhead through which a streak of sunshine came.

"I didn't do nothing much," he said finally. "My grandmother took and died and I wanted to drive down there to see her funeral."

"What happened?" I said.

He looked up at the window overhead and moved slowly across the cell until he could see a patch of blue sky.

"On the way down there I just stopped at the store and drank one little bottle of beer."

[162]

LOWELL, MASSACHUSETTS. You wonder who wears all those thousands of yards of cloth while you are catching up snapped warp threads. You would like to see your wife get a new dress out of it once in a while.

"I don't believe five per cent of the people in this country realize that two years from now we may be ducking into cellars and dodging bombs on a twenty-four-hour schedule. It's going to be a great shock to a lot of people if we wake up some morning to find ourselves at war. And it's that initial blow that's going to be the test for us. Right now there is not enough morale to withstand the shock, and the only way we can prepare for it is to jar the population into realizing what we will be up against if war does come. We need weekly black-out practice, transport mobilization practice, and conscription for home-defense practice. You can't get senators and congressmen to act, because in this democratic paradise they aren't sure what the majority of their constituents would say about it. We could be training civilian home guards in first aid, fire-fighting, and police duty. We could be forming mobile guards that could be rushed from one city to another on a moment's notice. We could be training those woodchopping, tree-planting CCC boys to man armored cars and speed boats in time of emergency. We could be doing a hundred things that ought to be done. But no, we sit around here on our rosy rumps

[164]

St. Johnsbury, Vermont.   The handcraftsman had a bad year because the girls he hired to pack toys talked so much they forgot and put too many parts in one box, not enough in others, and most of his orders were canceled.

day after day, doing nothing, while the advance lines of war creep silently upon us. We are not hypnotized. We are just plain dumb."

RESTLESS AMERICAN

The doctor picked up his appointment book and thumbed through it several times absent-mindedly. Then without paying particular attention to what he was doing he began tearing out the sheets page by page and throwing them into the wastebasket.

"I can't stick it out here any longer," he said nervously, getting up and crossing to the window.

He stood there looking down at the rainy-day traffic in the Washington street. After several moments he turned his back to the window.

"I'm closing up my office Monday," he said, glancing around the room. "I'm going into the Army. I'm a reserve officer in the medical corps."

He turned to the window once more and looked down into the rain-swept street.

"With all this going on these days, I can't sit in an office any longer. I've got to get right into the middle of things. I've got a twelve-thousand-a-year practice, but it doesn't mean a thing to me now. I've got to get out and get into the

[166]

St. Johnsbury, Vermont.   They still make playthings and wooden pails and pitchfork handles by hand, but they are afraid some day the machines will take away all the business.

thick of it. This is no place for me any longer—
I'm getting into the Army the first thing Monday
morning."

He came back to his desk and began digging
into stacks of correspondence, medical journals,
and bills. He glanced at half a dozen letters, and
then he swept the whole batch to the floor. He
got up and reached for his hat.

"Let's get out of here and see what's happening down on the street," he said. "I'm through
with private practice."

IT DOESN'T SEEM LIKE THE SAME OLD PLACE
    ANY MORE

I had walked seven or eight blocks looking for
a taxicab when I finally saw one standing idle.
There were plenty of taxis on the streets, but
Government workers, pouring from office buildings by the thousand, apparently had engaged
every available cab in Washington.

I ran to the vacant cab at the curb half a
block ahead. When I opened the door, the driver
did not look up. He was figuring on a pad of
paper.

"Sorry, buddy," he said. "No can do."

"Engaged?" I asked.

CHICAGO, ILLINOIS. Skyscraper girders, ball bearings, gun barrels, razor
blades, can openers, cam shafts, shell casings, plow points, watch springs,
armor plate, throttle valves, meat cleavers, molar drills.

"Sorry. No can do," he repeated without looking up.

I opened the door and sat down on the rear seat. He still did not look up.

"What's the matter?" I asked, leaning forward and looking at the papers on the seat beside him. "I've got to get to the Mayflower Hotel. How about running me over?"

The driver turned around and looked at me squarely in the eyes.

"Friend," he said, "I wish I could help you out, but I just can't spare the time. I've got to fill out these papers."

"What kind of papers?"

"Income tax," he said, waving a handful of papers before my eyes.

"You must be making a lot of money these days," I said.

"That's the trouble. I make too much money. I didn't use to make enough to pay the income tax, and now just look at me! I feel like a millionaire! I know how those rich birds feel now. Boy! Does it hurt to pay it out after you've made it!"

"There must be a lot of money being spent in Washington now," I said.

"That's only the beginning," he said. "This town's never seen so much money before. I'm

CEDAR RAPIDS, IOWA. After living with the smell of the weld and looking into a blue world of flying sparks all day long, it is good to push up your mask when the whistle blows and get ready to go home.

getting one- and five-dollar tips like I used to get dimes. That's how it is. But every time I get one of those tips I let out a groan, because I know I've got to be honest and put it down for the income tax. Believe me, it hurts!"

He turned around in his seat and looked at me for a moment.

"Imagine me!" he said, smiling. "Paying the income tax! A year ago I was down in Alabama sweeping up crumbs off the floor. And just look at me now! Paying the income tax!"

"Do you suppose you could run me over to the Mayflower when you finish making out your tax return?" I suggested.

The driver lit a cigarette and offered me one.

"This country doesn't seem like the same old place any more," he said, blowing smoke out the window. "Everybody's got plenty of money, and if he ain't got it, he knows where he can get it. It don't even seem like America any more. Remember back when we had the depression? That was when nobody had a dime, and people all over begged like low-down bums. Hell, no! This ain't America any more. This is some other place."

"If I could get to the Mayflower—" I began once more.

NEW YORK, NEW YORK.   There are always plenty of jobs for pastry cooks and dishwashers at the summer resort hotels, but nobody wants to go back to the country once he has come to the city to get a start in life.

"I'll tell you what I'll do," the driver said. "Here's my card. You take it up the street to the Willard Hotel and give it to the doorman. Make out like you are a guest there, and tell him you're a friend of mine. Taxis are too scarce this time of day for him to get one for just anybody, but if you give him my card and let on like you are a guest at the Willard, he'll do his best to find a taxi for you. If he asks about me, tell him I'm busy as hell making out the income tax."

NEW YORK, NEW YORK. Car hops and bobbin boys, auto courts and night shifts, hitch hikers and hotel greeters, beauty queens and bank nights, prayer services and union meetings, personal appearances and gossip columns, all-night movies and bunion derbies.

Photographing *"Say, is this the U.S.A."*

Starting out to collaborate with your husband on a new book, in this case our third, is like being married all over again. In order to achieve a successful collaboration, it is necessary to understand each other's ideas and feelings.

The quality that makes you useful as a collaborator is your method of following your own ideas, because photography is a specialized field and you should know what can and what cannot be done with it. But the thing that makes you still more useful as a collaborator is your understanding of the writer's conception so that you are carrying out his ideas in your own photographic way.

Working together with the same purpose in mind is essential, because even though one half of the team uses a typewriter and the other a lens, the two mediums must function congenially so they will come together and weld. Together they produce something quite different from the activities of either and build together something they could not construct separately.

Our object was to give the impression and feel of America. America is a big country and there are an infinite number of choices of subject matter. Other collaborators would make an entirely different set of choices and the result would be another impression of America. This was our impression, and we could go on forever adding to it, but it seemed practical to stop sometime.

The pictures were made throughout many trips here and there, taken throughout the past year, but the bulk of the photographs were taken on a fairly concentrated trip from the East Coast to the West Coast and back.

In our particular choice of places we often followed whimsical reasons —going to Pretty Prairie because we read a tiny item in a newspaper which first brought to our attention the fact that such a delightfully named place existed, and going to San Diego because in days past it had been our joy to go to night clubs there and watch the sailors dance. Sometimes our photographic stops had unforeseen consequences, as in

[176]

Tucson, where we fell so in love with the unbelievable giant cactus that we bought a ranch while our work went on.

In spite of these seeming whims, we always had a background plan. As each subject was finished, we proceeded to another geographical area, and chose a cast of characters that would portray an entirely different type of American citizen, so that in the end we could emerge with a pattern that would form the backbone of our book.

There is something about Kansas that makes it a rich field for the photographer of Americana. It is not only the center of America; it looks like the center of the country. Wheat farmers look like wheat farmers, grain elevators dot the landscape, and Oddfellows Lodges and Sewing Circles have a distinct this-is-the-middle-of-America flavor.

When we reached Kansas we wanted to start in on something that we thought was an integral part of that center-of-the-country feeling, so we chose a freight train, and spent several days with it. A passenger train, especially the streamlined variety that comes flashing through, pausing only to draw breath at large railway stations, would have been more glittering. But we chose the humble freight train, which we felt had not been honored enough, and which forms a vital connecting link throughout the Middle West. Everybody depends on it. Everything is carried in it.

We rode on top of the train to take pictures of the landscape—and it was a breezy place for a camera—as it rattled its way from one whistle stop to the next. We dismounted and watched and worked, while it unloaded sheep and cows; we loaded ourselves in again, while it picked up furniture and pipes. We sat on our heels in boxcars, we got acquainted with the crew and learned their picturesque slang names for each other, and we rode in that hallowed place, the caboose, where sometimes one finds delightful surprises—in this case, an art gallery.

Sometimes we would come on surprises that were difficult to arrange to photograph. While wandering through the Dakotas, on the watch for nothing more exotic than typical Dakota farm life, we heard people talk about the colonies of "Russians." The Hutterians, when we found them, turned out not to be Russians at all, but there was no doubt about their photogenic quality. Like actors from an Old World play, they moved

[177]

among their stone buildings, the men bearded, and the women and girls in long plaid or candy-striped dresses.

We were received hospitably, but when we got ready to take pictures, we found that it was against their religious beliefs to be photographed. Finally, the women, who were very friendly, discovered a technicality that could be turned to my aid. While it was against their religious code to have their pictures taken, they felt that this rule need not apply to those members who had not yet been baptized. Since Hutterian children are not baptized until a fairly advanced age, I had a large selection of models to choose from. I focussed happily on the unbaptized until the dinner bell rang out, when the women in charge of the community kitchen thought the governor, returning hungry, might put the spirit, if not the letter of the law, to too stern a test.

More often, however, it was not the exotic that attracted us, but the ordinary. Sometimes our subjects were so bread-and-butter that it was hard to find a beginning. But it was just this everyday quality that we wanted to capture, if we were to truly portray America.

In Provo, Utah, the town was characterized by a business-like, upstanding, moderately prosperous character, and the selection here of that thoroughly American institution, the Rotary Club, seemed to be appropriate.

In Texarkana, we found a spot where the activities of several regions come to a focus. To the south of it are oil wells, to the east is cotton, and to the west are the cattle plains. A crossroads like this is bound to be characterized by trading. Thus we felt that there was no better subject to illustrate it than horse-trading, that colorful, spirited maelstrom of droning auctioneers and stamping livestock and sharp buyers.

On our trips through America I carried five cameras, having among them twelve lenses. These were:

1. 3¼" x 4¼" Speed Graphic. A specially built job with interchangeable lenses ranging from 9 cm. to 30 cm., in focal length, and synchronized for flash work.

2. 3¼" x 4¼" Linhof view camera. With interchangeable lenses ranging from 7.50 cm. to 30 cm., and battery case and extensions for multiple-flash lighting.

3. 3¼″ x 4¼″ Soho reflex. An English camera of the Graflex type, but smaller and more flexible, and greatly preferable because of its tilting and twisting front board.

4. 2¼″ x 3¼″ Plaubel-Makina. With 3 interchangeable lenses, 7.3 cm., 10 cm., and 19 cm. The Plaubel has the advantage of taking packs, with their larger film size, instead of miniature film, even though the overall size of the camera is approximately that of the Contax. Also it has a built-in range-finder for quick focussing.

5. Fairchild Airplane Camera, taking twelve and one-half- or twenty-five-foot roll film, making negatives 5″ x 7″.

In the field of lenses, a variety of focal lengths is to the photographer what a large vocabulary is to the writer. The photographer who takes news or action shots should not have to be deprived of this advantage. Of course, he can change his lenses back and forth on the standard Graphic model, but that necessitates focussing on the ground glass, a procedure which at once nullifies those features of speed for which the Speed Graphic was intended. With this in mind, I had my Speed Graphic adjusted so that it would take the following five focal lengths: 9, 12.7, 15, 18, and 30 cms., and the bed has engraved footage scales for each.

The lenses are mounted in metal boards, numbered in red from one to five, and the infinity stops on the camera bed have been indicated by an engraved line which is correspondingly numbered in red so that the appropriate lens can be set at its proper point in an instant. Mounted on the top of the camera are two tubular view-finders. The right-hand view-finder is the standard one found on all Speed Graphics, but with a set of masks which can be slid into place to match the lens changes, so as to show the same field on the view-finder that the lens includes. The left-hand view-finder had to be specially calibrated to match the unusually long focal length of the 30 cm. telephoto. Instead of having only the usual right-hand range-finder, the camera is equipped with one on each side, set to handle respectively the most frequently used lenses, i.e., the 12.7 cm. Ektar and the 18 cm. Zeiss Tessar. The focussing for the remaining three lenses is handled by means of a Leitz range-finder set on top of the camera between the right- and left-hand view-finders.

[179]

With all these built-in gadgets the camera looks a little like a Lilliputian anti-aircraft position detector, and five months went into its construction. But the desired result has been achieved—that of combining the quick-working facilities of the Speed Graphic with the advantage of changing from one focal length to another, which seems so essential to me if the best possibilities of design and composition are to be brought out of each subject.

This camera, for instance, was of great use in a place like the livestock auction, where mules were stamping all over the place, a constant peril to photographers and horse-traders alike. The three legs of a tripod would have increased the hazards, and decreased the chances of catching those swift-fleeting things like the gesturing of the auctioneer bellowing out his bids, the changing expressions on the faces of the bidders, and the glimpse of a buyer looking into the horse's mouth, so that you feel, for a second, that the man is not examining the horse, but that the horse is looking over the teeth of his future master.

When it comes to a picture that can be composed and lighted more carefully, there is no equal, in my opinion, to a small flexible-view camera, used on a tripod. This can be synchronized with flash bulbs, employed never from one source, which would result in flat lighting, but employed from extensions so that multiple flashes can be set off simultaneously from several sources. The Linhof, which forms part of this equipment, has the same film size as the Graphic, and has tilting and twisting back and tilting front, a great aid in composition and focussing. All possible features have been made interchangeable with the Graphic; lenses and lensboards, view-finder masks, filmpack adapters, battery cases, wiring, and all units of the flash equipment. The camera has been mounted with view-finders that match those of the Graphic, and has been equipped with right-hand and left-hand range-finders, so that in an emergency, it also can be used in much the same way as the Speed is used.

The Soho I find especially useful for portrait or action work out-of-doors, like the girl with the lasso, where her swinging rope had to be stopped at a 1/800th second, or like the tractor moving through the wheat field, where the tilting front made it possible to keep in focus the wheat close to the camera (by pushing the top of the front board out), and at the same time keep the tractor, which was further away, and the still more distant clouds, in focus all at the same time with a minimum stopping-down of aperture. The picture of the long line of ROTC boys illustrates the value of the Soho's side-twisting front board, which helps to equalize the plane of focus when the near figure is almost at the photographer's elbow, and the end of the column is a hundred feet down the field. If this focus were maintained with the rigid-fronted Graflex, the lens would be stopped down so far that the exposure would have to be lengthened until it would be impossible to catch the fluttering flag without blurring it.

When some American manufacturer awakens to the usefulness in the reflex camera of this simple and flexible device, there will be many happier American photographers.

The Plaubel was kept at hand when casual strolls in the streets made a heavier and more conspicuous camera undesirable. Its aperture speed of 2.9 was helpful in fading light, and this camera was also fitted with flash equipment for which I carried midget bulbs, to use when poor daylight needed to be supplemented by an occasional flash. The possibility of using larger than miniature-size film with resulting better quality for reproductions, combined with the camera's miniature size, is its greatest asset.

The Fairchild was used for the airplane pictures, which were taken from a small cabin plane, from which the doors had been removed so that I could shoot out freely, while a machine gunner's belt held me in place. In the case of the wheat field pictures, the pilot took me into the air the instant the sun passed the horizon, because it was important to get these photographs while the rays of the sun reached the fields at an extreme slant, otherwise the perfectly level landscape would be flattened out to a degree unsuitable for airplane photography. In this case we were at work even before the hardworking Kansas farmers, and we had to circle around above their roof tops until we saw them come out and start their tractors and hook up their horses.

It is important in airplane photography to work with a pilot who un-

[181]

derstands what a photographer is after, and who has the skill to maneuver a plane with facility so the photographer can catch the exact composition he wants for his picture. Here I had a barnstormer with whom stunt-flying was a livelihood, and his long practice in clearing pylons at races and diving into bright-colored balloons at county fairs, resulted in some astonishing maneuvers over combines and barnyards. At our altitude, however, the camera did not record the amazement that must have been registered by the farmers and mules below us.

M. B.-W.